W9-BNN-763

Stikky™ Night Skies

Stikky™ Night Skies

LEARN 6 CONSTELLATIONS, 4 STARS, A PLANET, A GALAXY, AND
HOW TO NAVIGATE AT NIGHT—IN ONE HOUR, GUARANTEED.

LAURENCE HOLT BOOKS
New York

© 2003 Laurence Holt Books
www.stikky.com

Distributed in the United States by:
Four Walls Eight Windows
39 West 14th Street, Room 503
New York, NY, 10011
www.4w8w.com

First printing January 2003.

All rights reserved. No part of this book may be reproduced,
stored in a data base or other retrieval system, or transmitted in
any form, by any means, including mechanical, electronic,
photocopying, recording, or otherwise, without the prior written
permission of the publisher.

Library of Congress Cataloging-in-Publication Data on file.

Cover design and illustrations by Kate Shannon.

ISBN 1-56858-253-6

10 9 8 7 6 5 4 3 2

Printed in Canada

What this book is about

Stikky Night Skies uses a unique learning method to introduce anyone who is interested to the stars of the night sky, step-by-step.

Each step builds on what came before and reinforces it. That way, by the time you reach the end of the book, you will be confident in finding your way around much of the sky.

Still more exciting, what you learn will serve as 'hooks' that you can hang future learning on.

The book also teaches you how to find which direction is north by reading the stars, so you will be able to navigate at night without a compass.

Stikky Night Skies has four parts:

- **Sequence One** introduces the constellation *Orion* and its famous star *Betelgeuse*, constellations *Cassiopeia* and the *Big Dipper*, and tells you where to look for planets in the sky. It also teaches you how to find the star *Polaris* and use it to figure out which way is north. *You should read this sequence in one sitting if possible.*

- **Sequence Two** builds on what you have learned in Sequence One, adding constellations *Cygnus*, *Taurus* and the *Pleiades*, stars *Sirius* and *Vega*, and the *Milky Way* galaxy. *Ideally, you should leave a few days, but no more than a week, between completing Sequence One and reading Sequence Two.*

- The **Epilogue**, a special feature of Stikky books, brings together everything you have learned and reinforces it in some new and unfamiliar situations. *Again, you should leave a few days between completing Sequence Two and reading the Epilogue.*

- If, by the end of the book, you are hungry to find out more, as we hope you will be, you will find dozens of things to explore in the **Next Steps** section.

You can skip to the Next Steps section at any time, of course, but the rest of the book only makes sense if read in order: Sequence One, Sequence Two, Epilogue.

How to read this book

Learning with *Stikky Night Skies* may be different from how you are used to learning. Please read this page carefully.

First, read Sequence One which runs from the next page to the **Pause point** on page 121. That should take only 30 minutes (but don't worry if it takes longer).

We find people get more out of the book if they stop there and practice what they have learned in the real night sky. We'd like you to do the same.

Then, after a few days, read Sequence Two. If you are away from the book for more than a week, you may find it helpful to review some of Sequence One before starting Sequence Two.

To get the most from *Stikky Night Skies*:

- Relax and take your time
- Don't worry about taking notes
- Don't worry about memorizing anything
- Try to avoid being interrupted.

Most importantly, by turning this page you promise yourself that, when asked a question in the text you will not flip ahead until you have tried to answer it.

(Flipping backwards to review pages you have already covered is fine.)

Keep this promise and what you learn will stick.

Sequence One

Take a look at the
night sky.

It has followed you
your whole life.

Brilliant minds
throughout history
have contemplated it.

Ptolemy, Galileo,
Newton, Einstein.

For thousands of years,
long sea journeys were
impossible without it.

One type of finch even
appears to navigate by it.

It's where we came from.
We all are made of star stuff.

You would not have gotten
far in ancient times without
knowing your way around
the night sky.

Indeed, it may be the only
thing your distant ancestors
would recognize today.

But do you recognize much
of it?

Or is it just so many stars?

About 30 minutes from now
you will recognize plenty.

Ready?

This is Orion.

Take a good look at him.

Orion's belt is one of the most
easily identified
features in the sky.

It's one of the few places
with three stars in a line.

Orion is the night sky's hunter.

Here is his body,

his shield,

and the club in his right
hand (he's facing you),
which will prove
important later.

The star at his right
armpit is Betelgeuse
(pronounced like "beetle
juice").

In real life it looks redder
than other stars.

It's at right angles to
Orion's belt.

Betelgeuse could end its life in a supernova explosion in the near future.

(By 'near future' cosmologists mean anytime in the next ten thousand years —so don't wait up.)

So, do you have Orion
fixed in your head?

Sure?

(Constellations change their
orientation during the night.)

Okay, find Orion's belt
before flipping the page.

Find his belt again.

Too easy?

Try his shield.

Now find Betelgeuse.

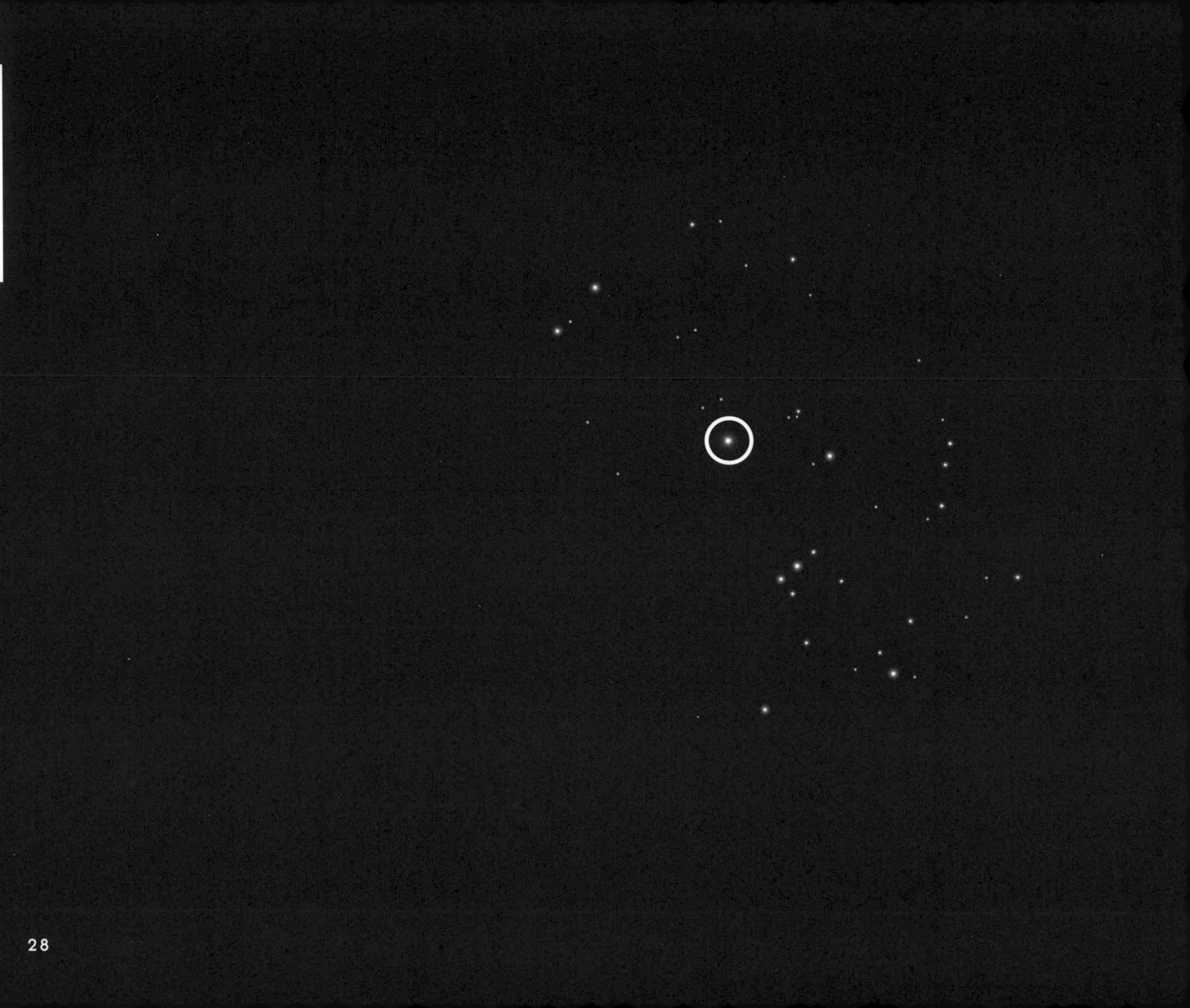

Constellations are just a
shorthand way of finding
your way around the sky.

This is more like the real
sky. Find Orion's belt again.

A bigger piece of sky.

Find Orion's body.

Now find his belt.

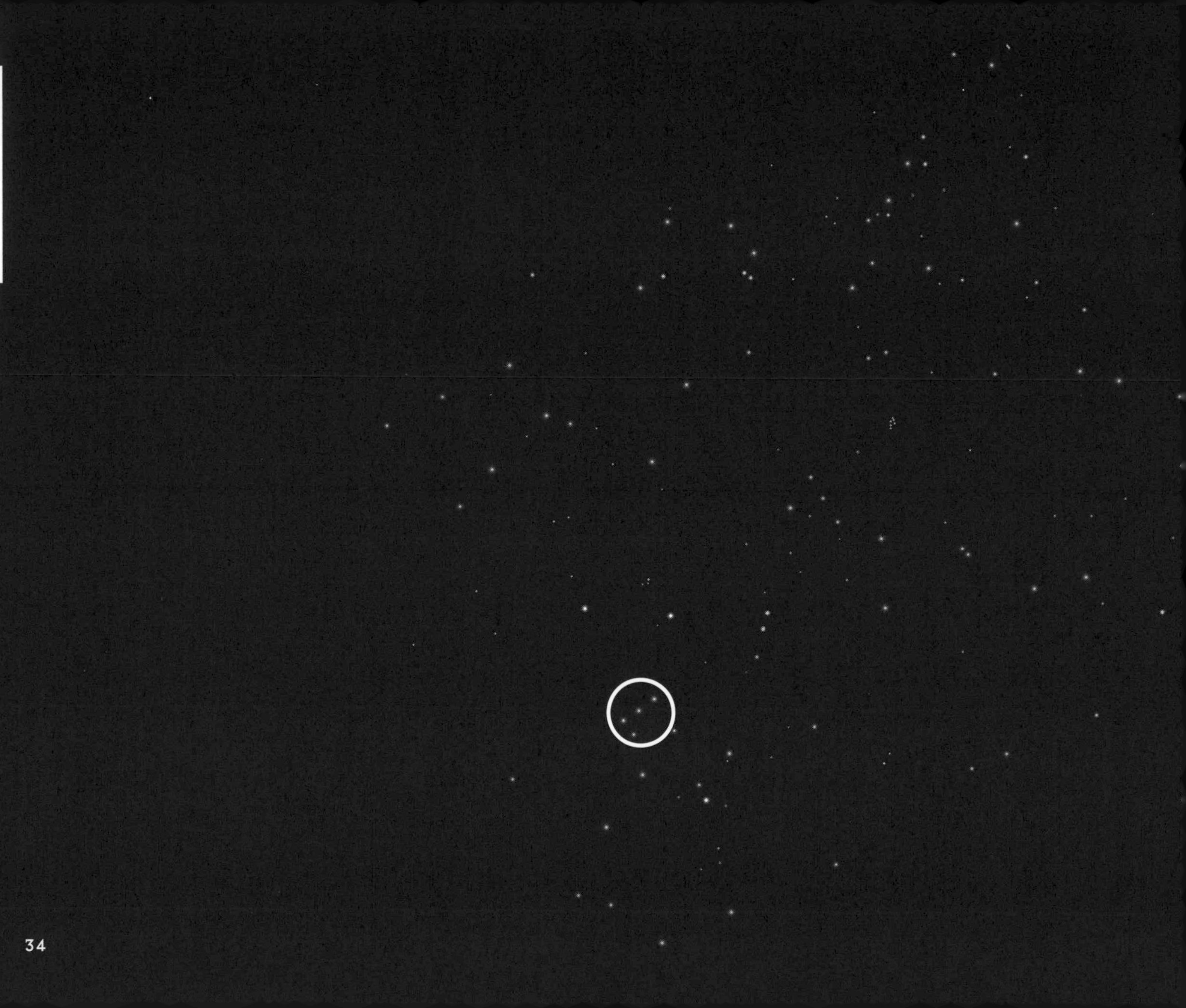

Getting tougher now.
Find Orion.

Don't flip the page
until you find it (unless
you really have to).

Find Orion again.

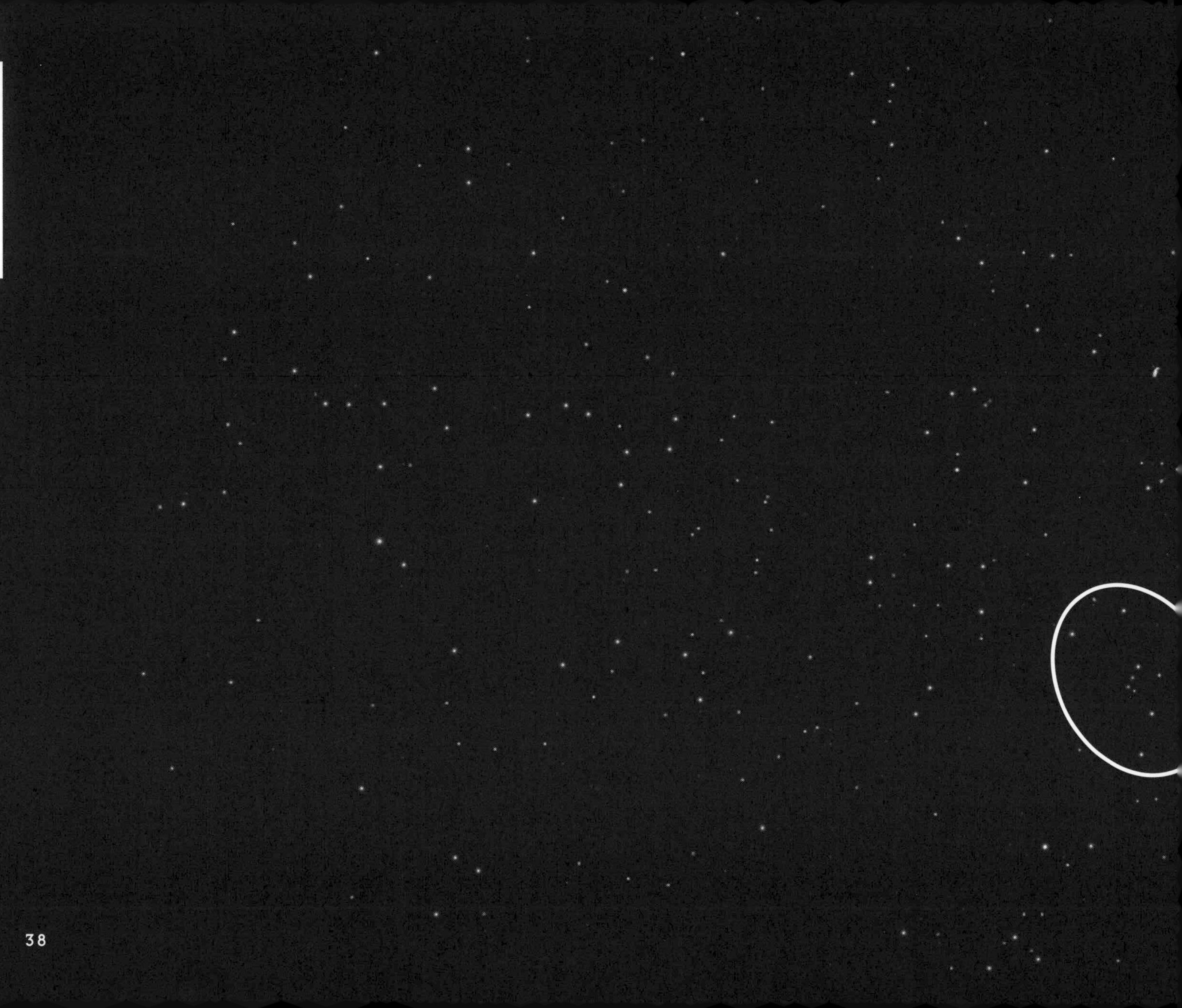

Find Betelgeuse.

In cities, you see fewer
stars due to glare from
lights on the ground.

Find Orion now.

Back to the countryside.

Where is Orion?

This is more as the
ancients would have seen
things. (They had fewer
street lights.)

Find Orion again.
Take your time.

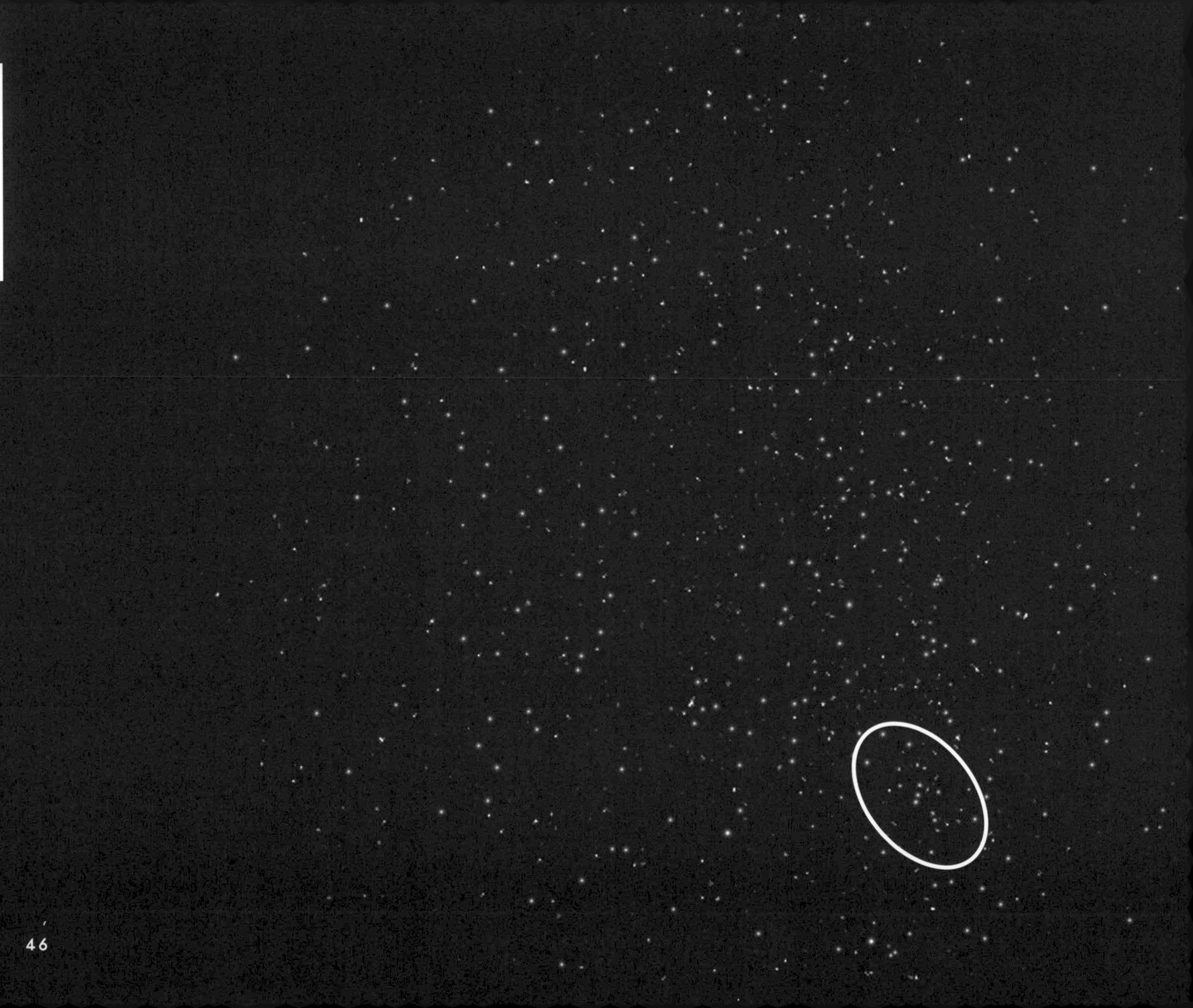

Find Betelgeuse.

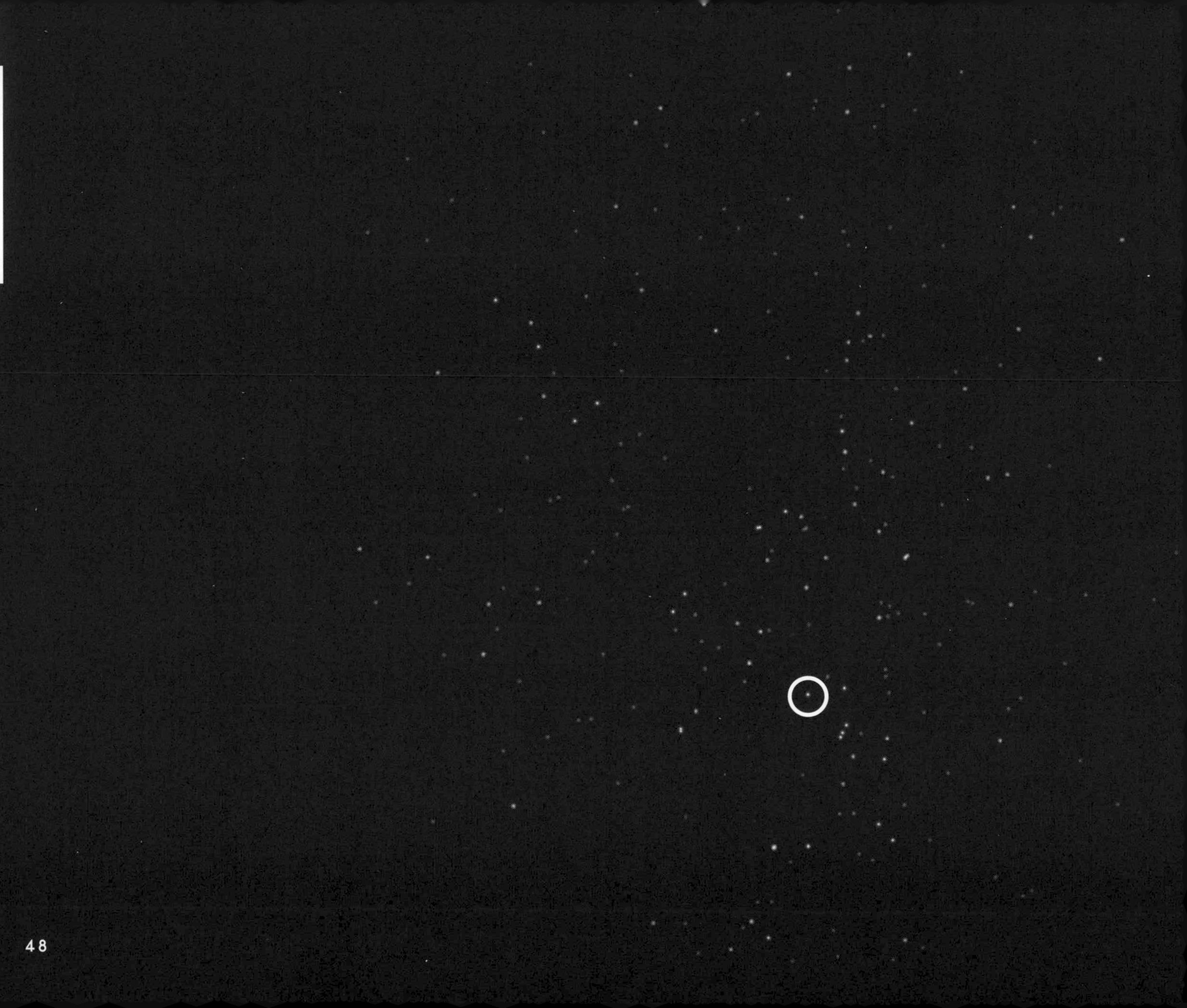

Betelgeuse again.

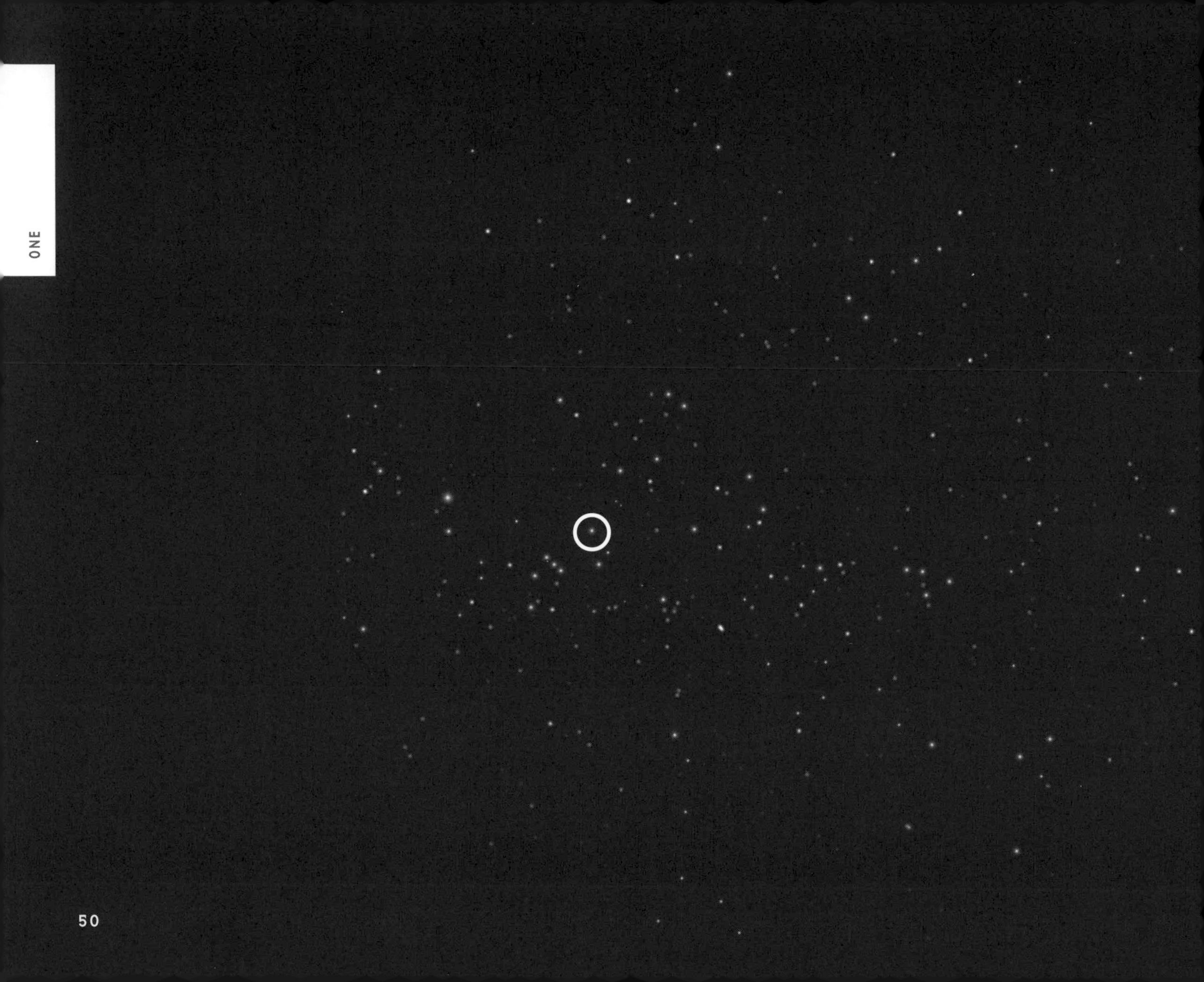

You just correctly
identified a single star
from over 300.

Time for another star group. This one you may know: the Big Dipper.

In Hinduism, these seven stars represent seven ancient sages.

It has a cup-shaped part
for dipping,

and a handle.

Okay, so find the Big Dipper
in this piece of sky.

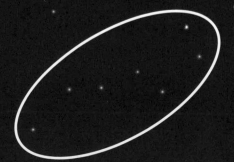

Find the Big Dipper here.

(Remember, the sky
rotates during the night.)

The Big Dipper has a very
interesting feature, as
you're about to find out.

So it's important you can
find it. If you are unsure,
you may want to go back
over the last few pages.

The two stars at the front
of the cup part of the
Big Dipper point to a star
called Polaris.

And Polaris is interesting because the whole sky appears to rotate around it.

(Actually, it's the Earth that rotates, but the effect is the same.)

A lot of people think
Polaris is the brightest star
in the sky.

But it isn't. In fact, it only
just makes the top 50.

Got Polaris fixed in
your head?

(Follow the front of the
Big Dipper cup.)

Still got it?

Okay, find Polaris.

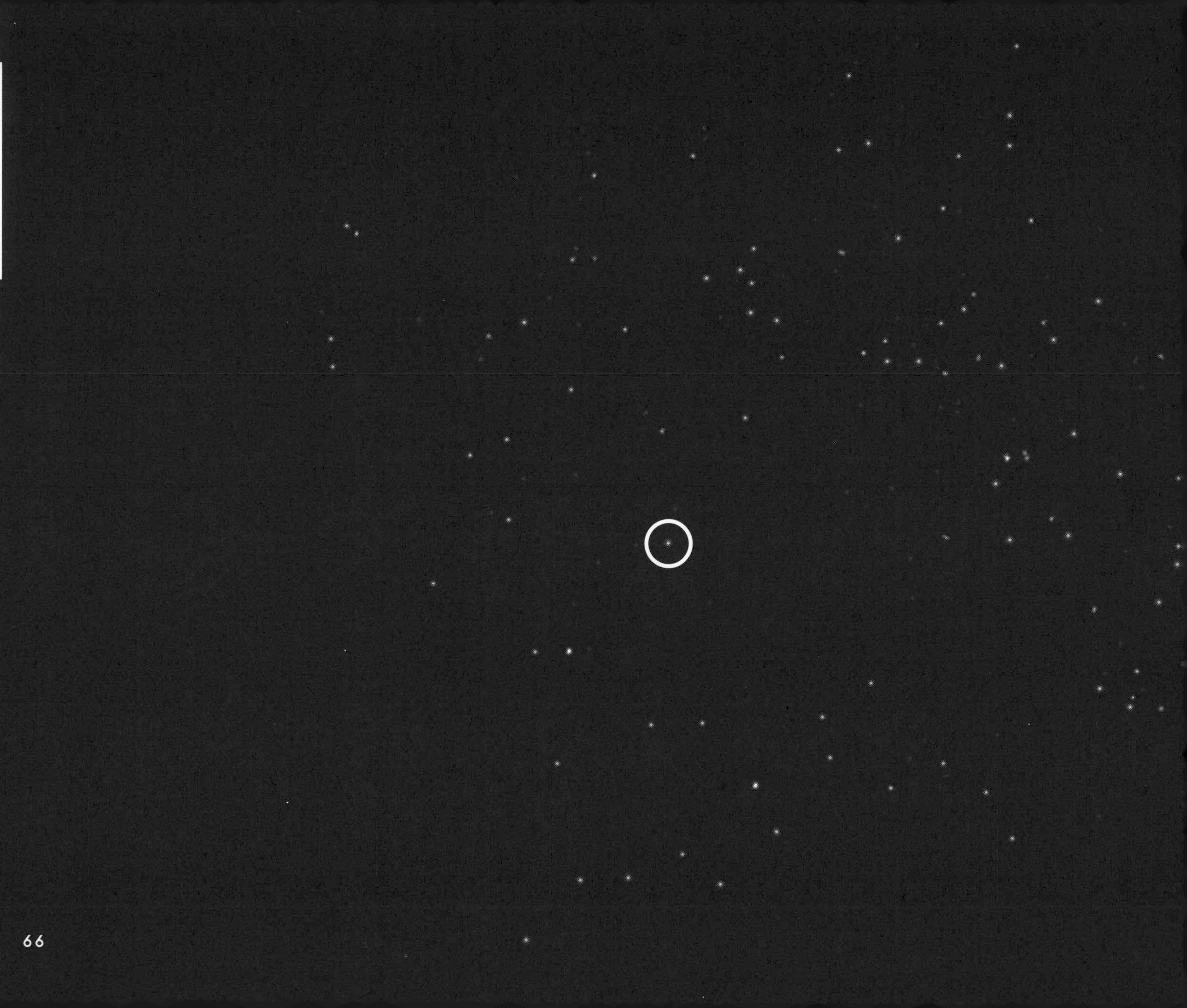

If you know where Polaris is,
you can figure out which way
is north…

Imagine the ⊕
symbol is the part of the
sky directly over your head.

Now trace a line from there
to Polaris.

The part of the sky directly over your hea

The line points north.

The part of the sky directly over your head

N

During the American Civil War, this is how fugitive slaves found their escape to Canada.

N

Your turn.

First, find the Big Dipper.

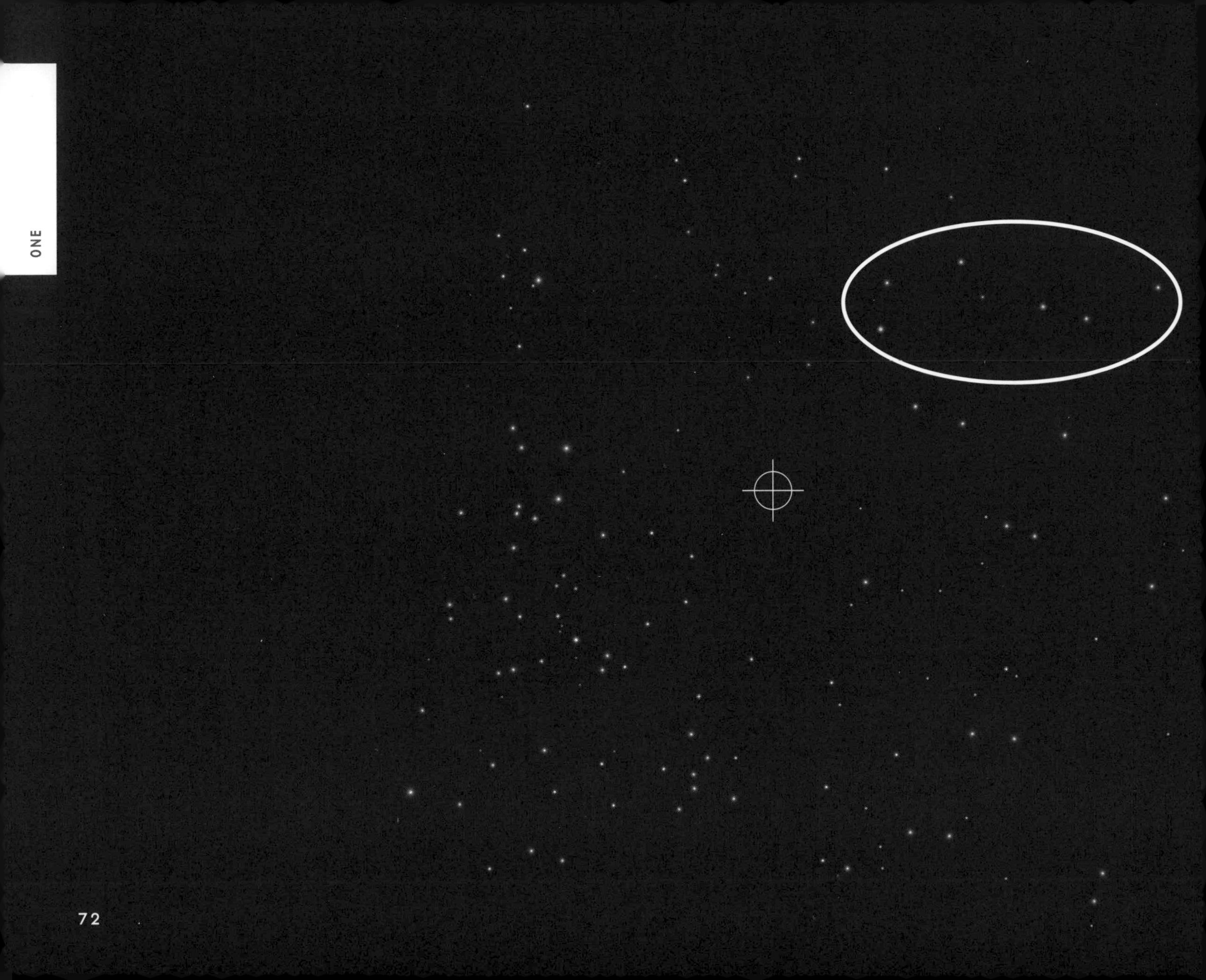

Now find Polaris.

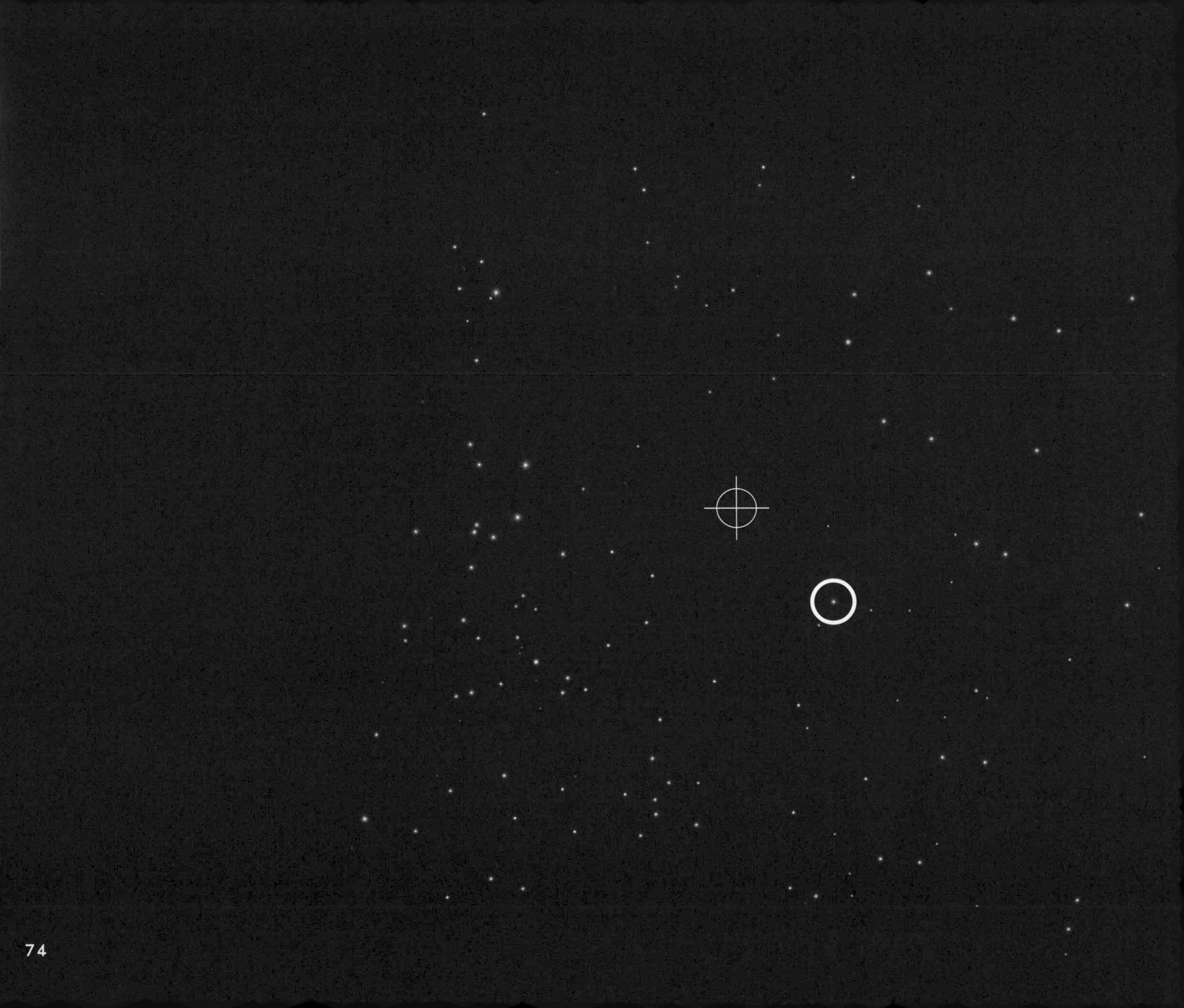

So which of these four
crosses is to the north?

(If you didn't get it, take
the time to go back and
figure out why.)

Here is a new piece of
sky. Find the Big
Dipper again.

Which is north?

Which is north now?

(No flipping, figure
it out first!)

If you made it this far successfully, you are a night navigator.

Congratulations.

Incidentally, this 'm' or
'w'-shaped constellation
is Cassiopeia ("kassio-
pee-a")—the queen
of Ethiopia in Greek
mythology.

If you squint, it looks
a little like a crown.

(Admittedly, you have
to squint a lot.)

Cassiopeia is always on
the opposite side of
Polaris to the
Big Dipper.

(Opposite the handle
part, not the cup.)

Polaris

So find Cassiopeia.

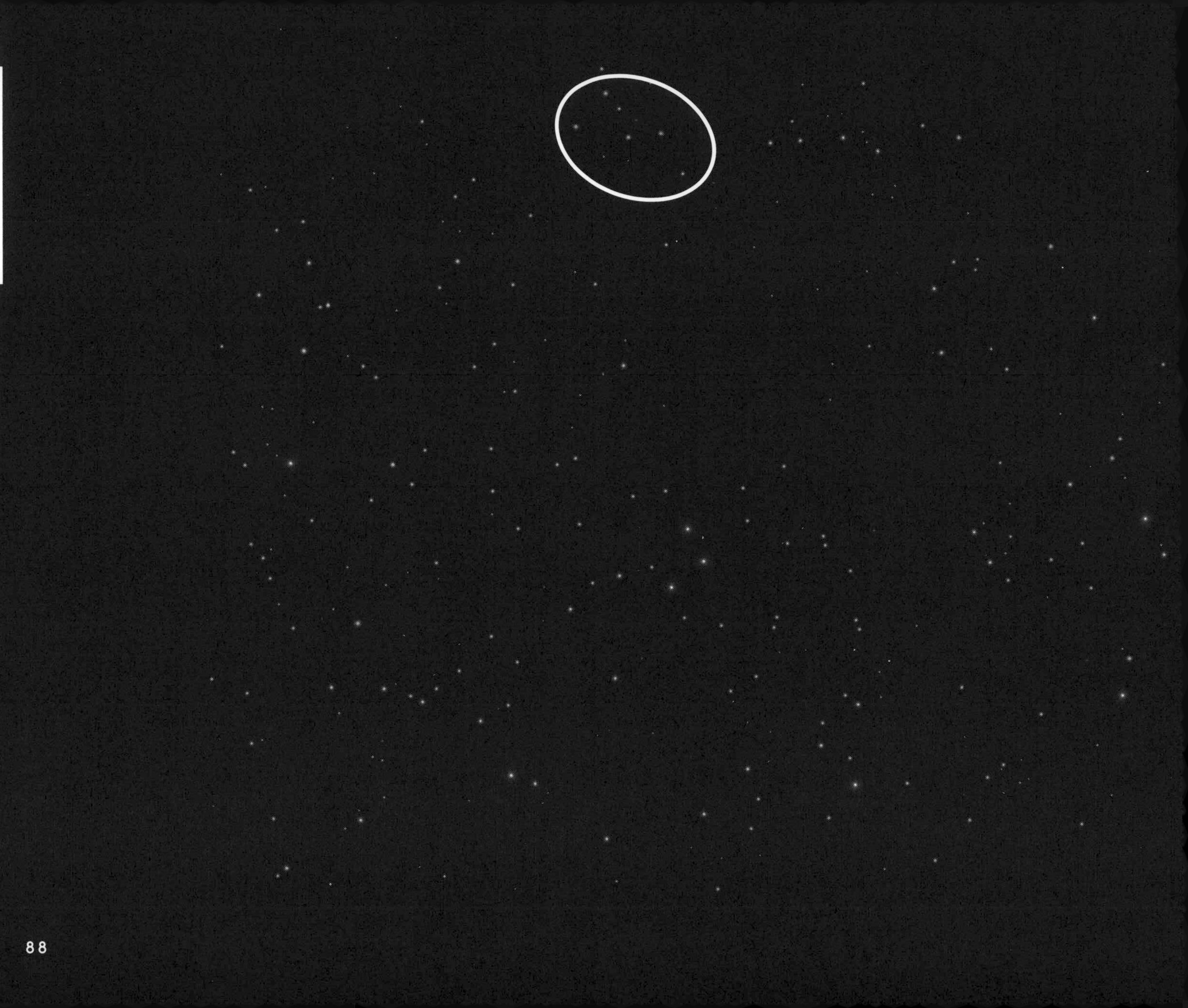

Find the Big Dipper.

(Clue: sometimes not all
the stars in a constellation
are visible.)

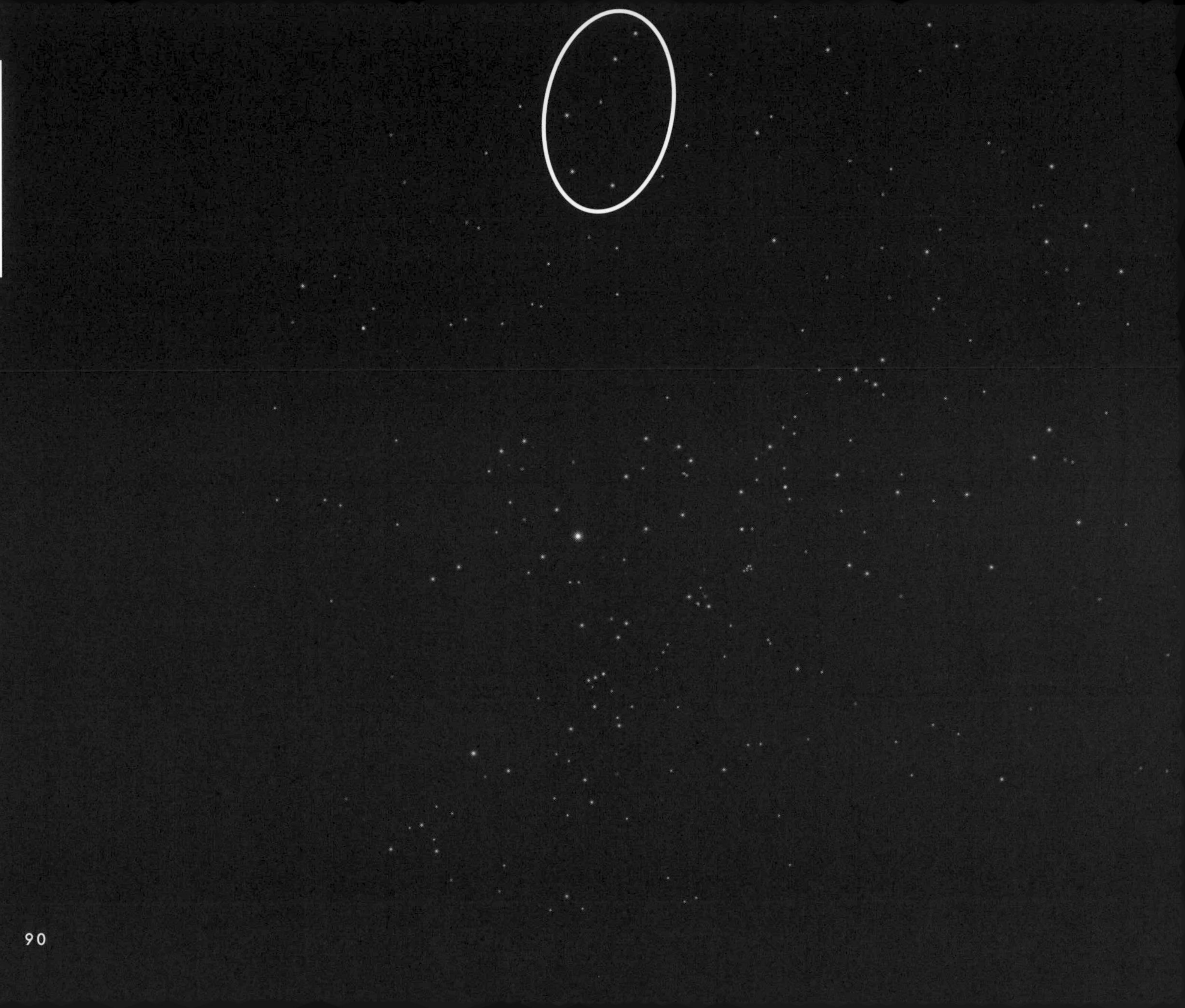

Where is Cassiopeia?

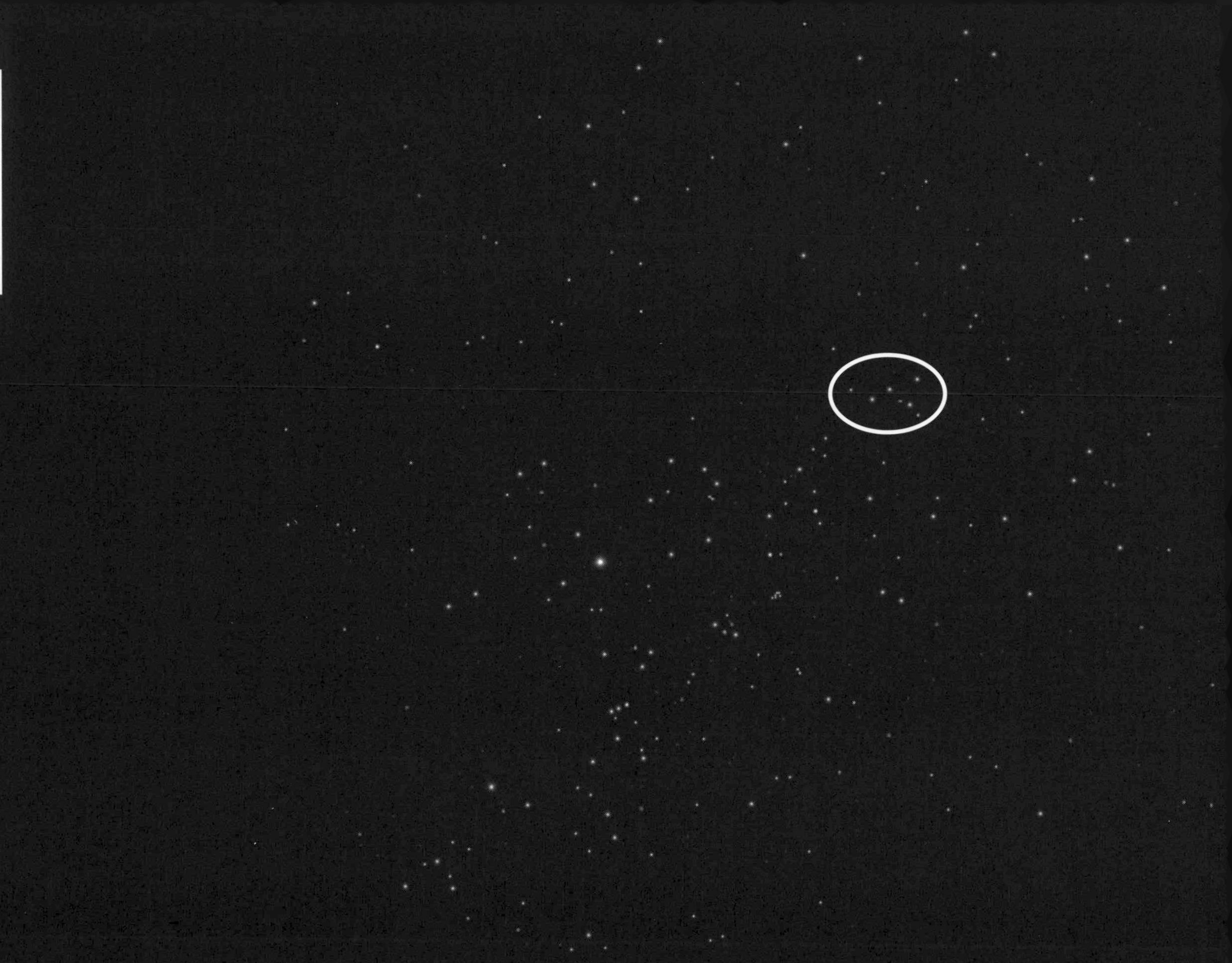

And a little recap.
Where is Orion?

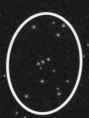

Betelgeuse?

'Betelgeuse', by the
way, is Arabic for
'the armpit of Orion'.

Remember the club in Orion's
right arm (he's facing us)?

Sometimes near the top of
it you'll see what looks like
a really bright star.

Actually, this is no star.

If it's brighter than anything else (except the Moon of course) it must be either Venus or Jupiter.

All the planets in our
solar system move around
a flat disk.

That makes
them easy to
find if you know
where Orion is
—they only move
along this line.

Don't worry about how to find this 'planet line' —we'll cover that later.

The finale to Sequence
One. If you're unsure
about anything so far,
you may want to go
back and review it now.

When you're ready,
start by finding Orion.

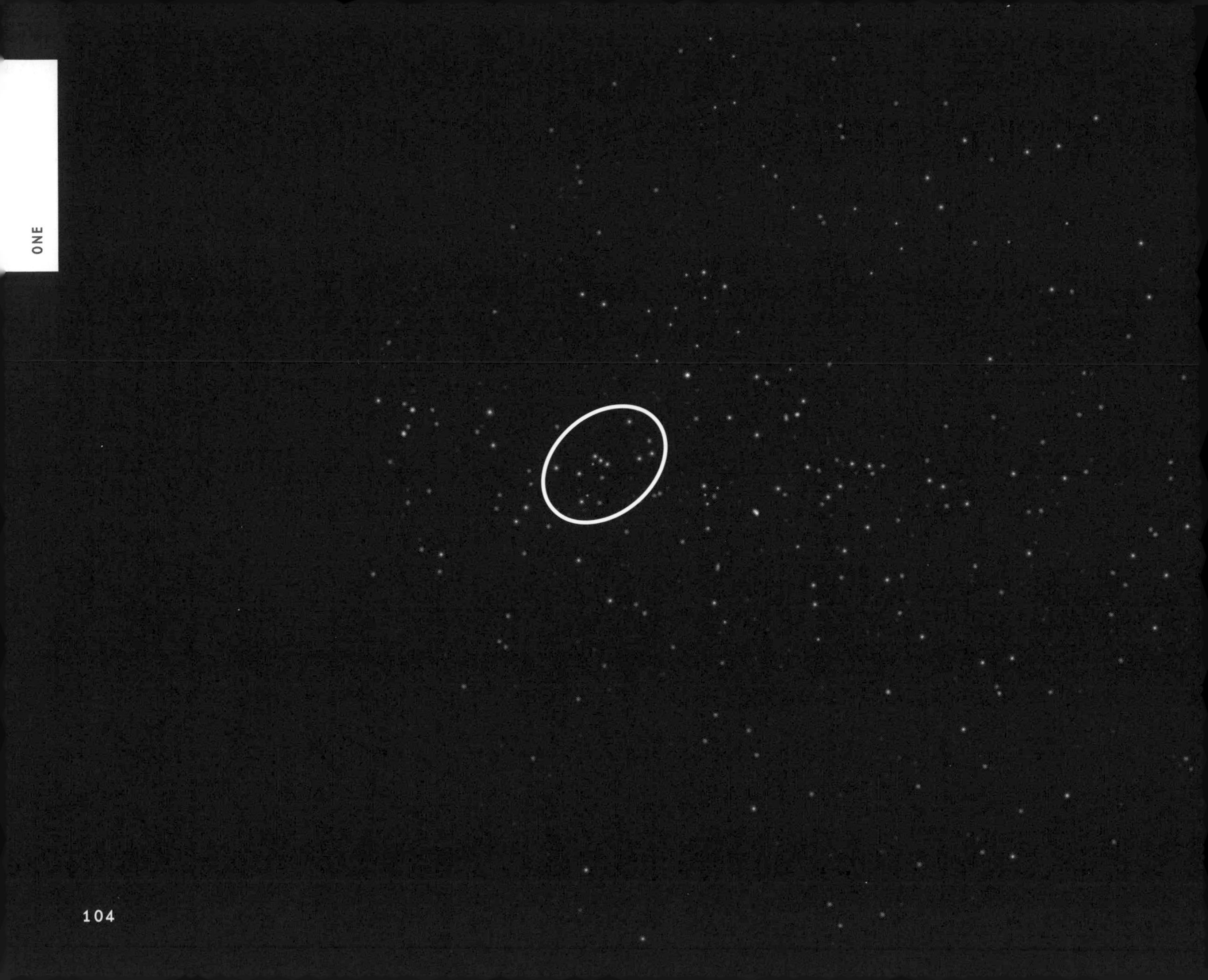

The Big Dipper.

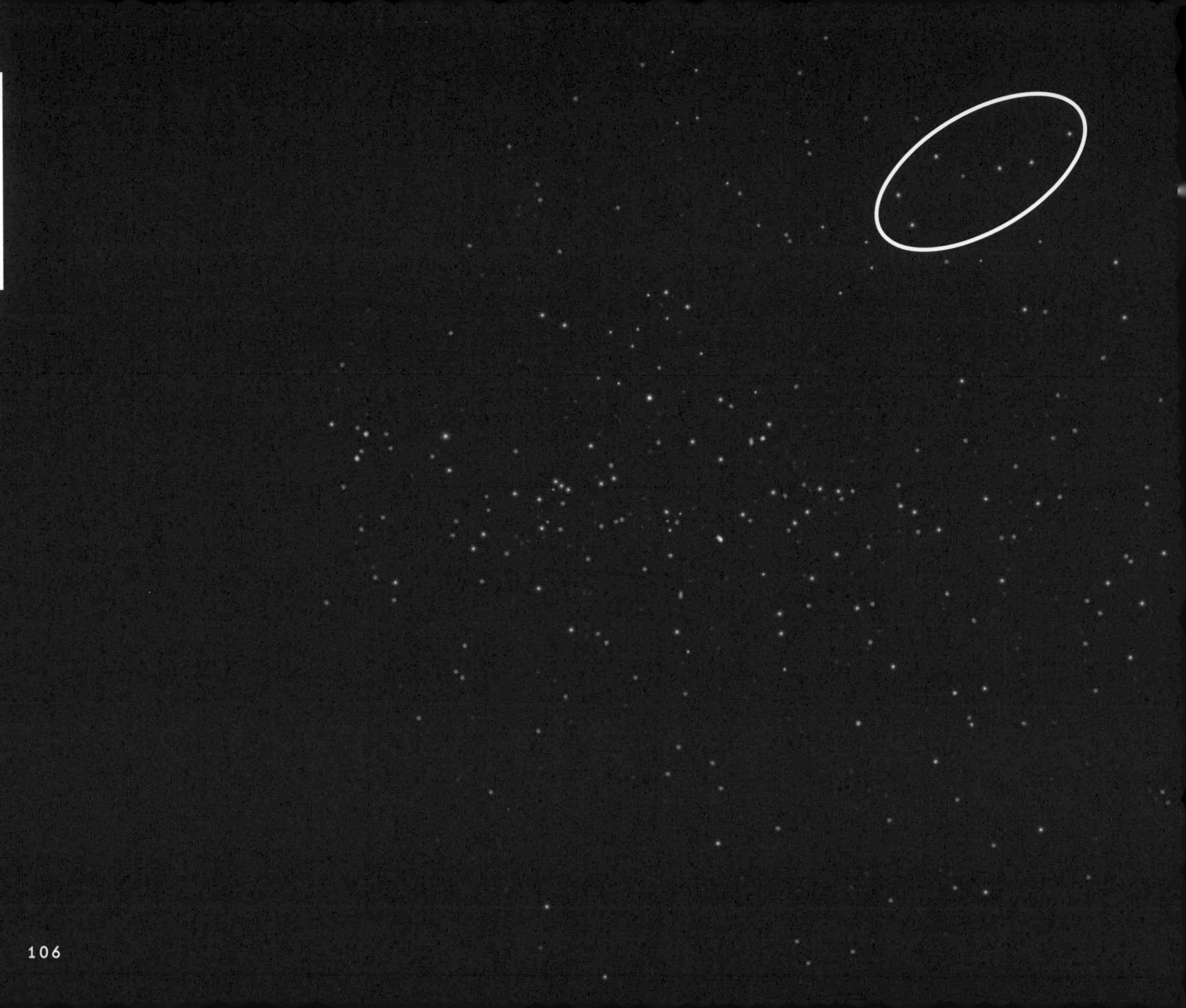

Now find Cassiopeia.

108

A planet (it happens to
be Venus).

The ancient Maya were
obsessed with Venus.
They built their calendar
around its 584-day year.

Now find Polaris.

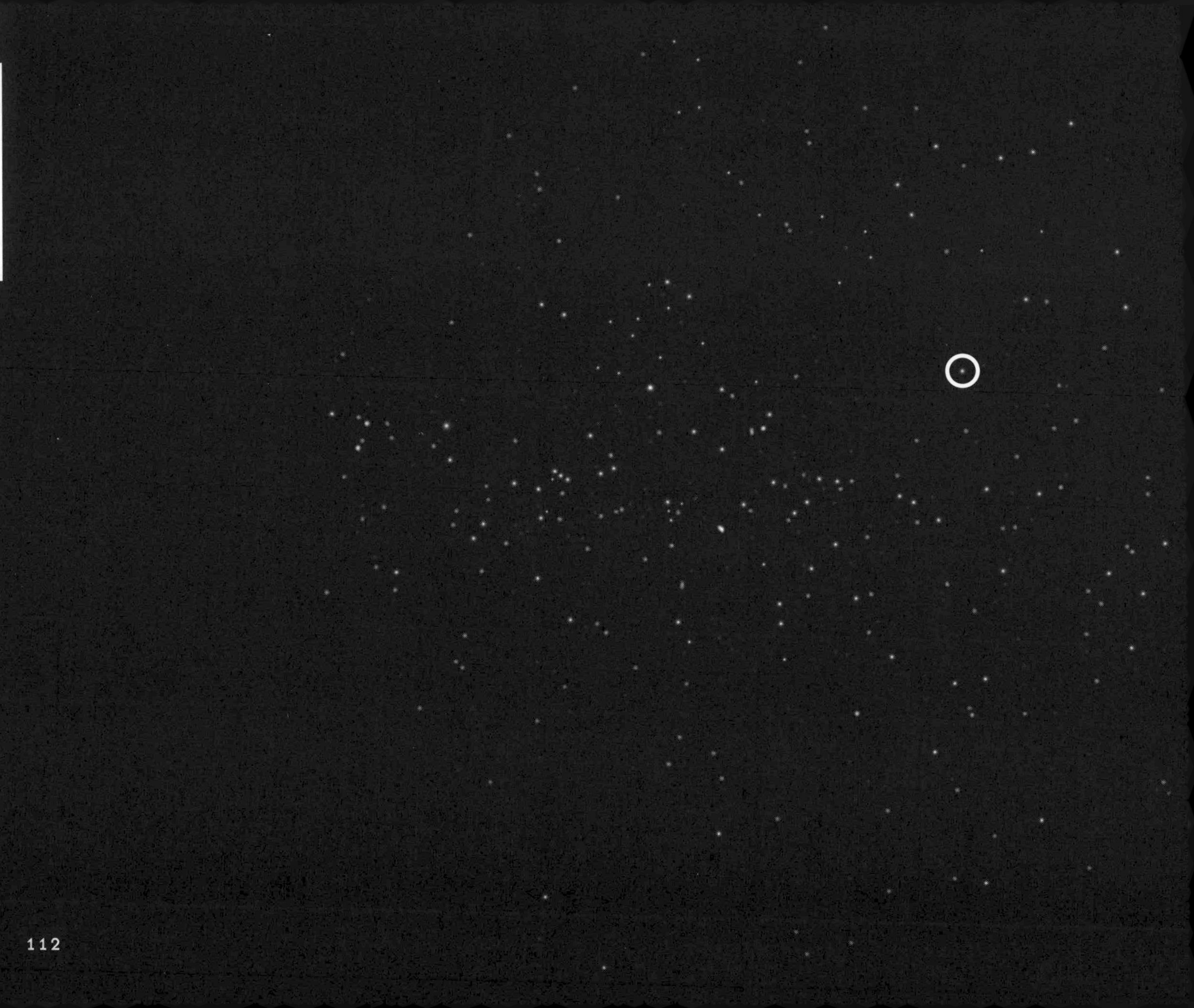

So which of these
crosses is to the north?

ONE

114

Finally, where is Betelgeuse?

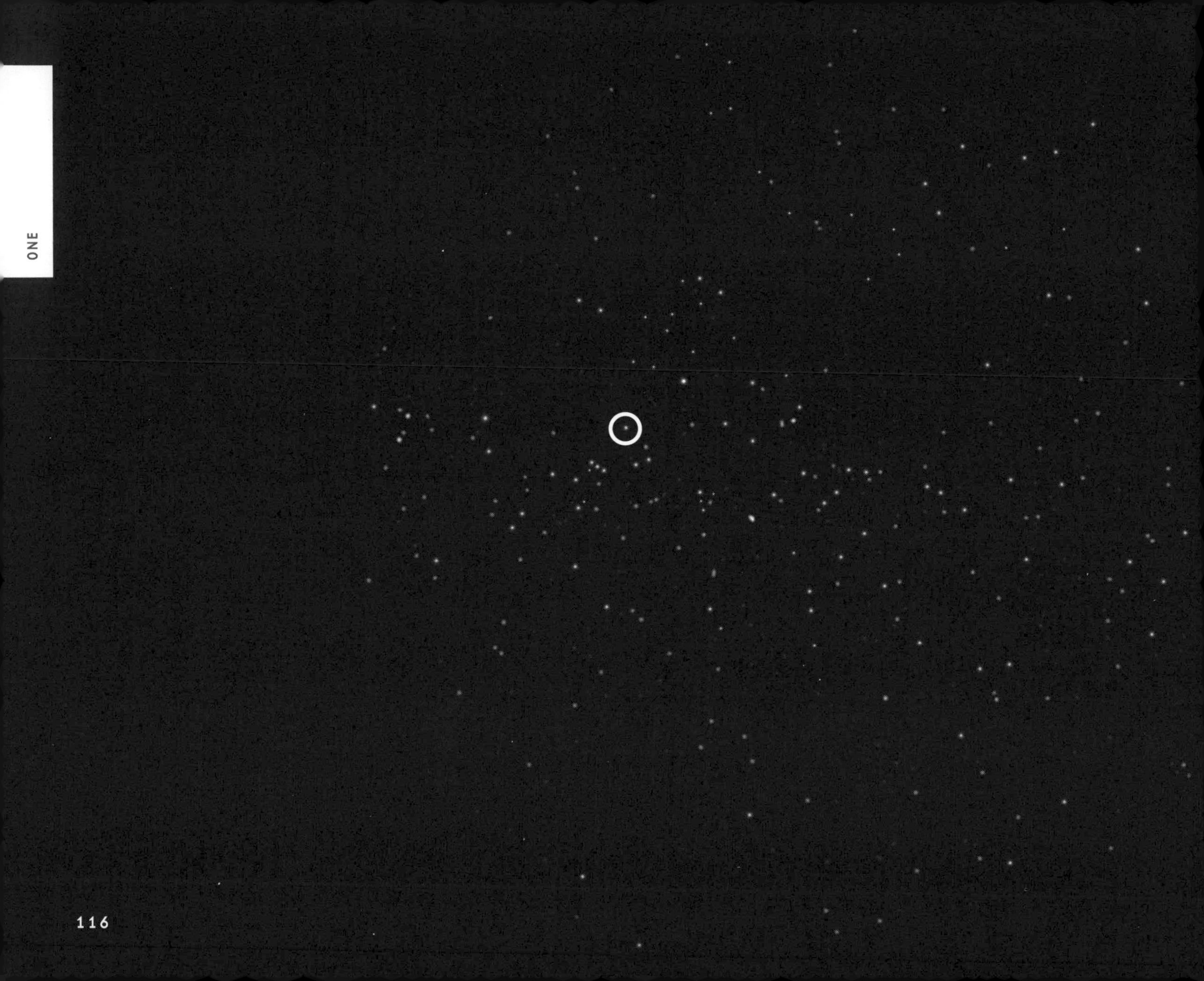

Congratulations!

You are now a
full-fledged
star gazer and
night navigator.

But your new skills
will fade unless you try
them out in the real
sky within a week.

If they do fade, just run
through this sequence again.

Have fun. And say "Hi"
to Betelgeuse from us.

Pause point

To get the most from this book, you should pause here.
This page explains why.

There's much more to come—but be sure to stop here and return to the book a few days later. Here's why.

In the days after you learn something new, your memory fades. You may forget most of what you learned. That might seem annoying, but imagine if you remembered everything you had seen only once; your memory would quickly become overcrowded.

So how do you prevent fading? You need to *reinforce* what you want to remember. The best way to reinforce knowledge is simple: use it. That's why we recommend going out on a cloudless night in the next few days and practicing in the real sky.

Then come back to *Stikky Night Skies* and start at Sequence Two on the page after this one.

If you are away from the book for more than a week, or if you don't get a chance to practice in between, you will want to review the end of Sequence One before starting Sequence Two.

(We have found that, when readers continue straight on to Sequence Two, they often get stuck and don't complete it, or find that they forget what they have learned more quickly.)

When you're ready to continue, read from the next page to the **Pause point** at the end of Sequence Two on page 193.

And remember your promise: when asked a question in the text you will not flip ahead without attempting to answer it.

Sequence Two

Included in this sequence:
more constellations, the
brightest star in the sky,
and what the inhabitants of
Los Angeles saw in the sky
after the 1994 earthquake.

But first a brief recap.

Find the Big Dipper.

Now find Polaris, the
North Star.

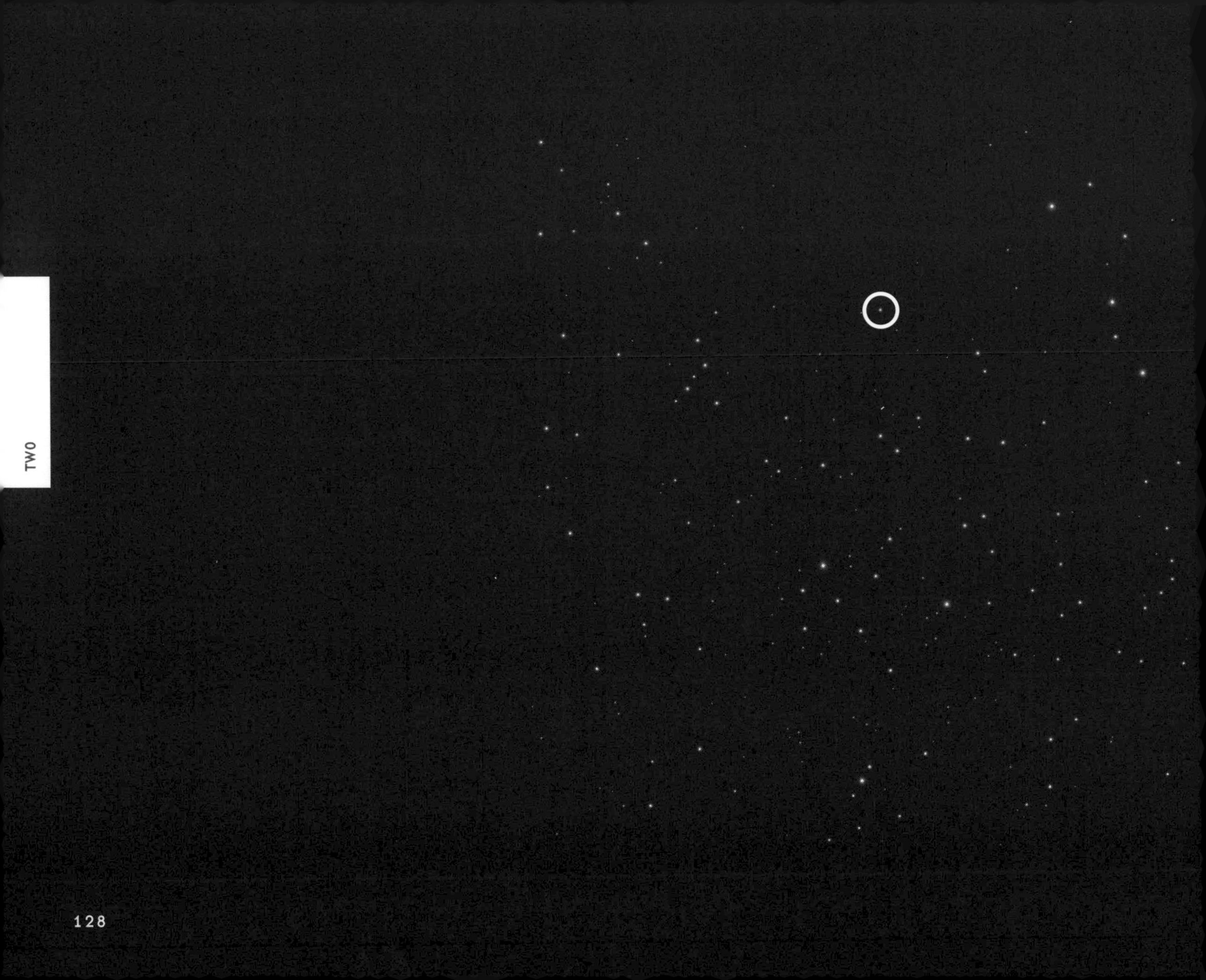

And Cassiopeia.

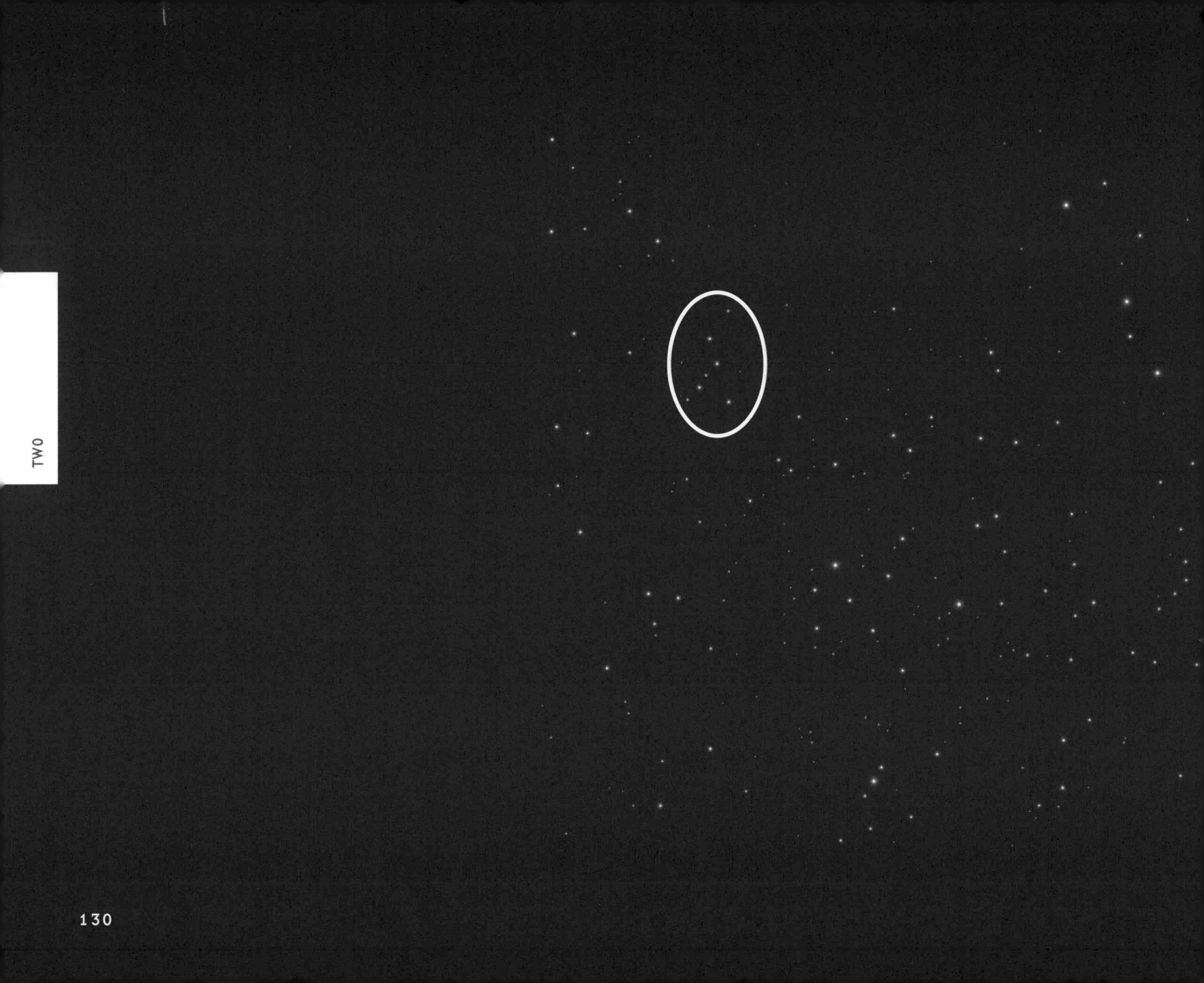

This simple cross shape is Cygnus which means 'the swan' in Latin.

Follow the three bright
stars in Cassiopeia to
find a wing of Cygnus.

(If you're not sure which
side of Cassiopeia to look,
try both.)

Some of the stars in Cygnus
are less bright, so it's a
tougher constellation to find.
In the real sky, it's easier once
your eyes have become
accustomed to the dark.

Here are his wings,

his neck,

and his tail.

In the Cygnus myth,
Zeus turned himself into
a swan in a bizarre attempt
to seduce Leda, queen of
Sparta. It worked.

Cygnus is important
since he'll help us find
something astounding
in a moment.

Try finding Cygnus in
this sky.

Remember, just follow
the three bright stars in
Cassiopeia.

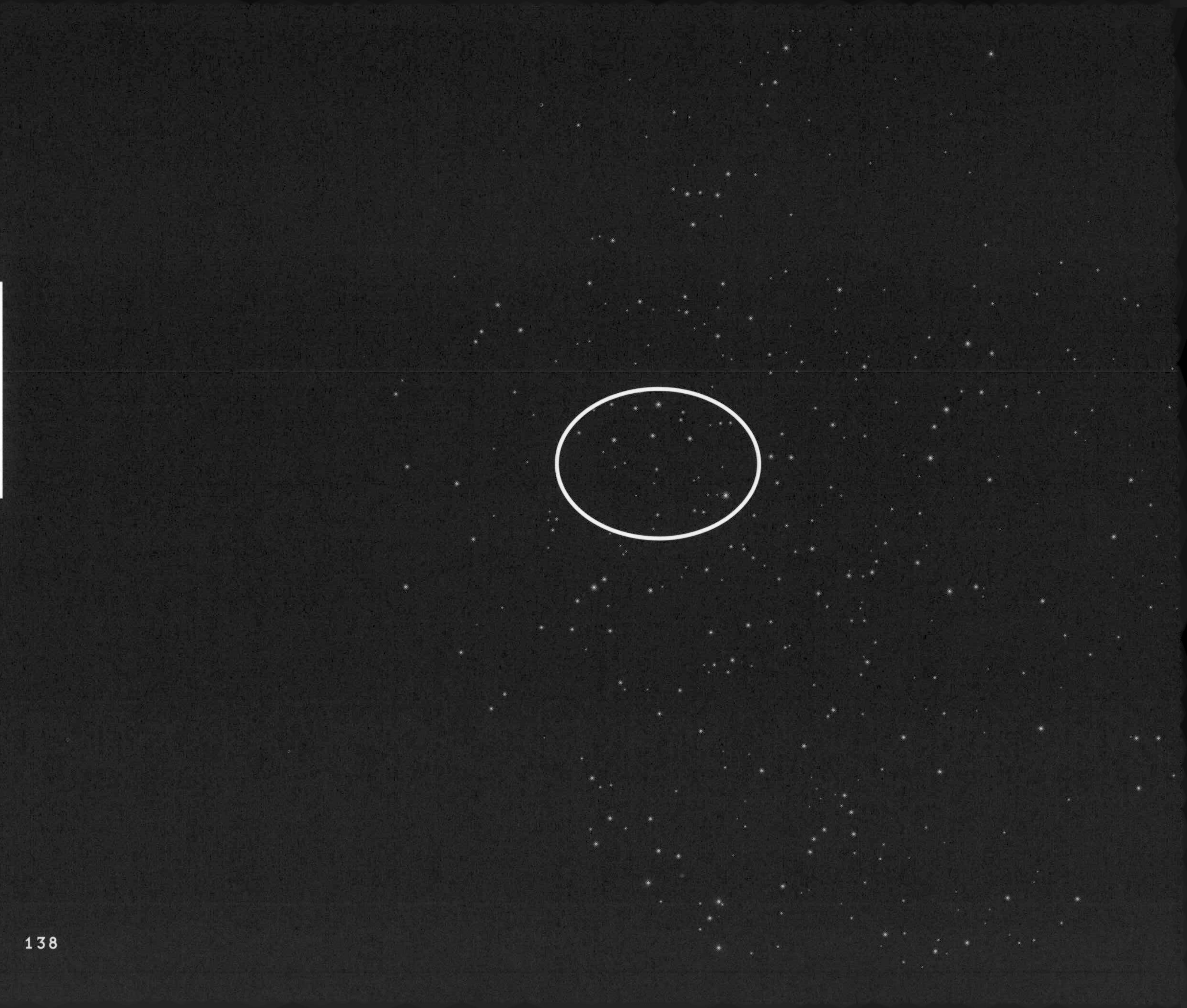

And here.

Possibly the most
remarkable feature of the
sky is also the toughest to
see with the naked eye.

You'll need a moonless
night, away from the glare
of the city.

But you'll be rewarded
with an incredible band
of faint stars across the
sky, running through
Cassiopeia and Cygnus.

This is a galaxy called
the Milky Way.

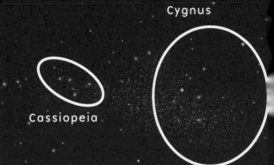

Cygnus

Cassiopeia

Find the Milky Way
in this sky.

(Again, remember
that the sky rotates
during the night.)

A galaxy is an enormous
collection of stars—over
100 billion in the case of
the Milky Way. Our Sun
is one of them.

And there are another
100 billion galaxies
out there.

Today, light pollution means
that, if you have seen the Milky
Way, you are in the minority.

In 1994, after an earthquake,
inhabitants of Los Angeles
called radio stations to report a
strange silvery cloud in the sky.

The earthquake had knocked
out the city lights so people
could see the Milky Way, many
of them for the first time.

While we're looking in this area—notice Vega (not Vegas), one of the brightest stars in the sky, above Cygnus's wing.

Vega is the standard for brightness and color used by professionals to judge all other stars.

Try finding Vega in this sky.

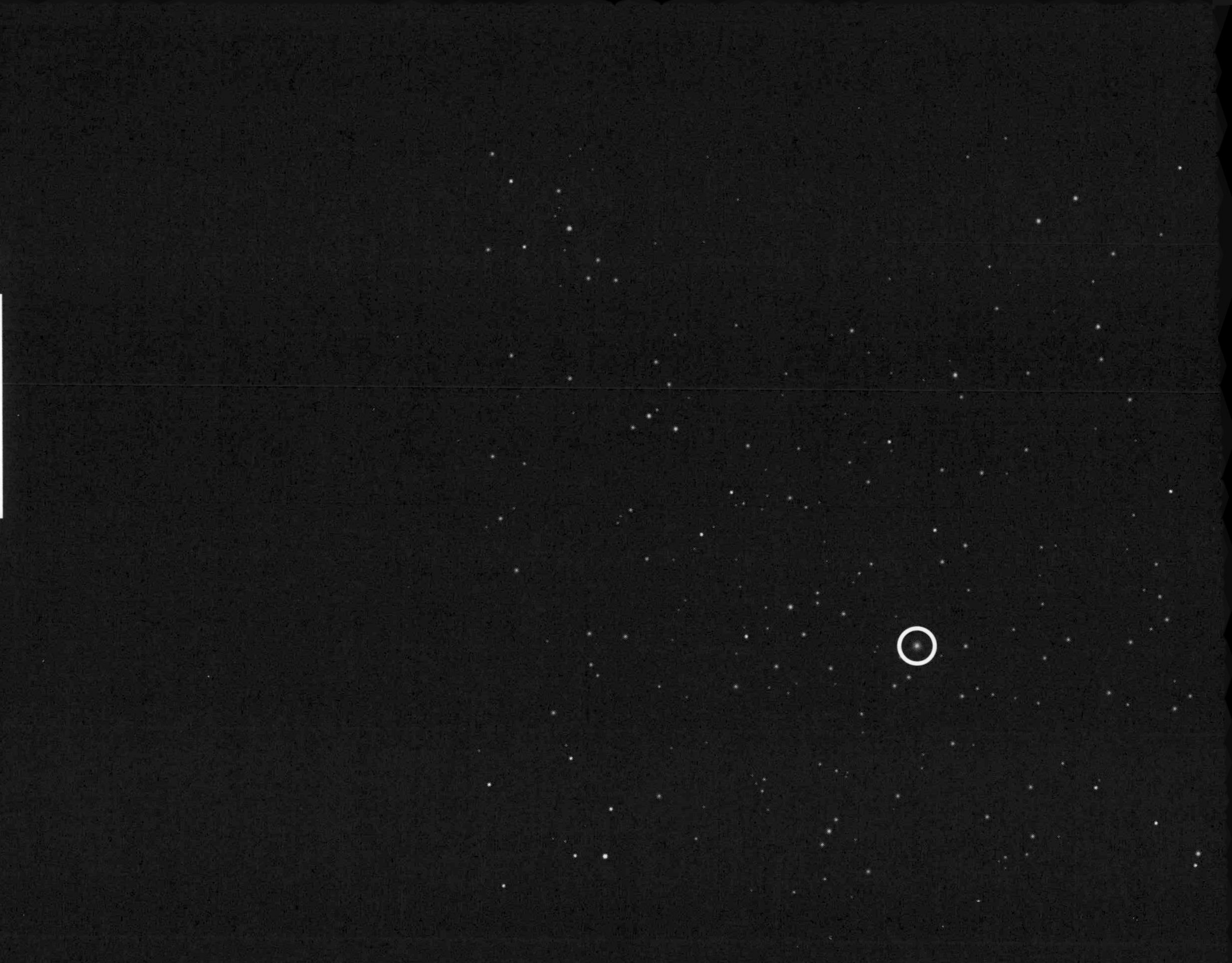

Now find Cassiopeia,
Cygnus and Vega.

Cassiopeia

Cygnus

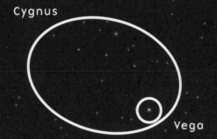

Vega

Where would the Milky Way
be if it were visible in this sky?

Okay, a new sky.

There's a familiar
constellation here. Which
star in it is Betelgeuse?

154

Orion has two bright
neighbors.

Follow his belt behind him
to find Sirius, the Dog Star.

Sirius is a very interesting star.

It is both the brightest star in the sky and the nearest star that is visible to the naked eye (other than the Sun).

In front of Orion is the constellation Taurus ('the bull' in Latin). During the night, as the sky rotates, Taurus moves across it pursued by Orion and his dog, Sirius.

(Okay, so you have to use some imagination.)

You can recognize Taurus by
it's 'V' shape—the bull's face.

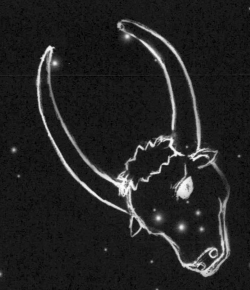

Find Sirius in this sky.

Find Taurus.

Find Taurus in this
fuller sky.

164

The other side of Taurus
from Orion lies many
people's favorite night
sky feature—a cluster of
stars called the Pleiades
(like "plee-a-deez").

The Pleiades may be one
of the first sky objects
mapped by man.

In 1940, in the caves
of Lascaux in France,
cave paintings were
discovered that appear to
include a 16,000-year-
old map of the Pleiades.

The Pleiades is also
known as the Seven
Sisters, though here it
just looks like a smudge
and in the real sky
you'll do well to pick
out more than six stars
in the group.

TWO

Here it is close up.

In Japanese, Pleiades is
'Subaru'. Check out the
car logo sometime.

Find Taurus in this sky.

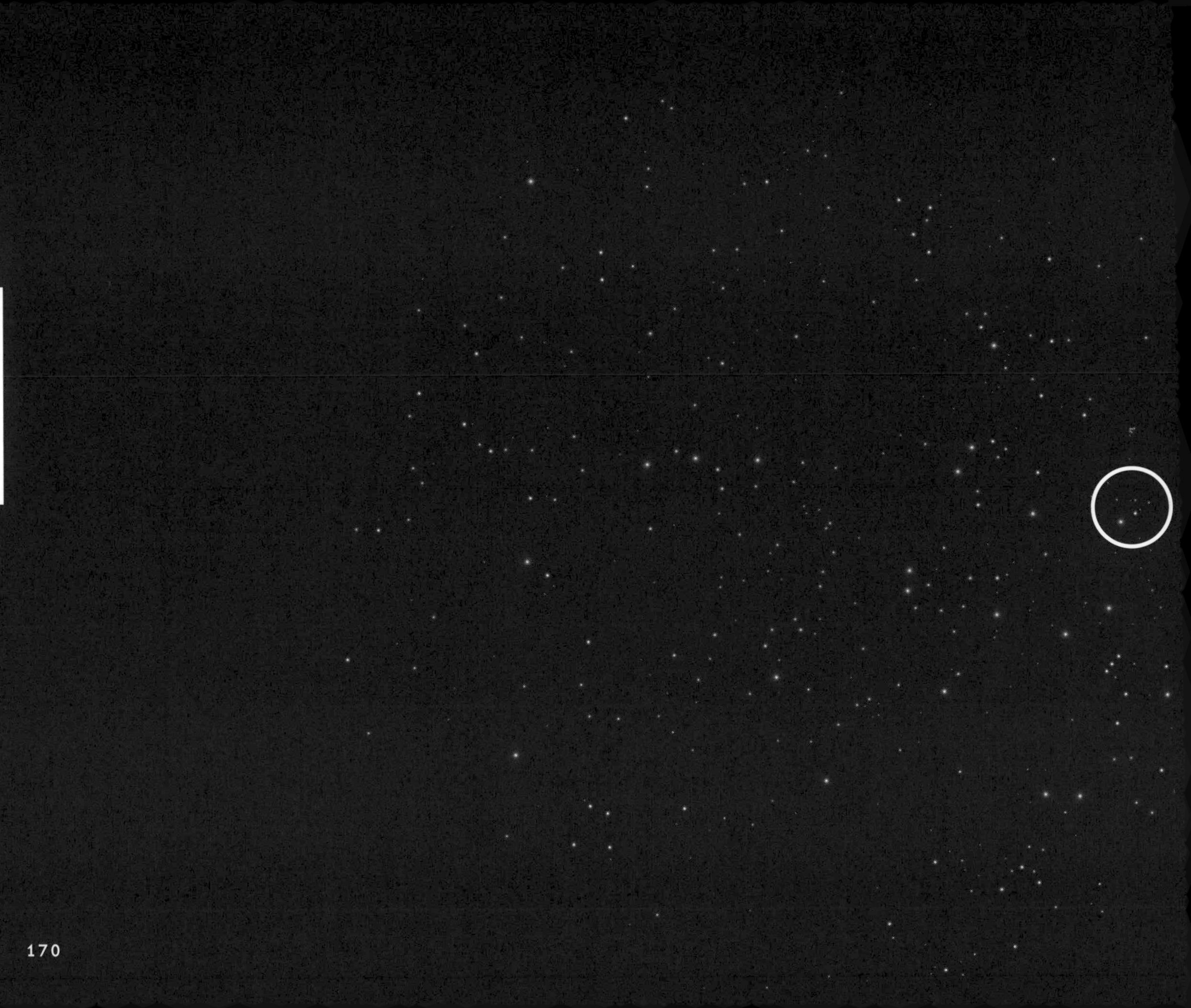

Now find the Pleiades.

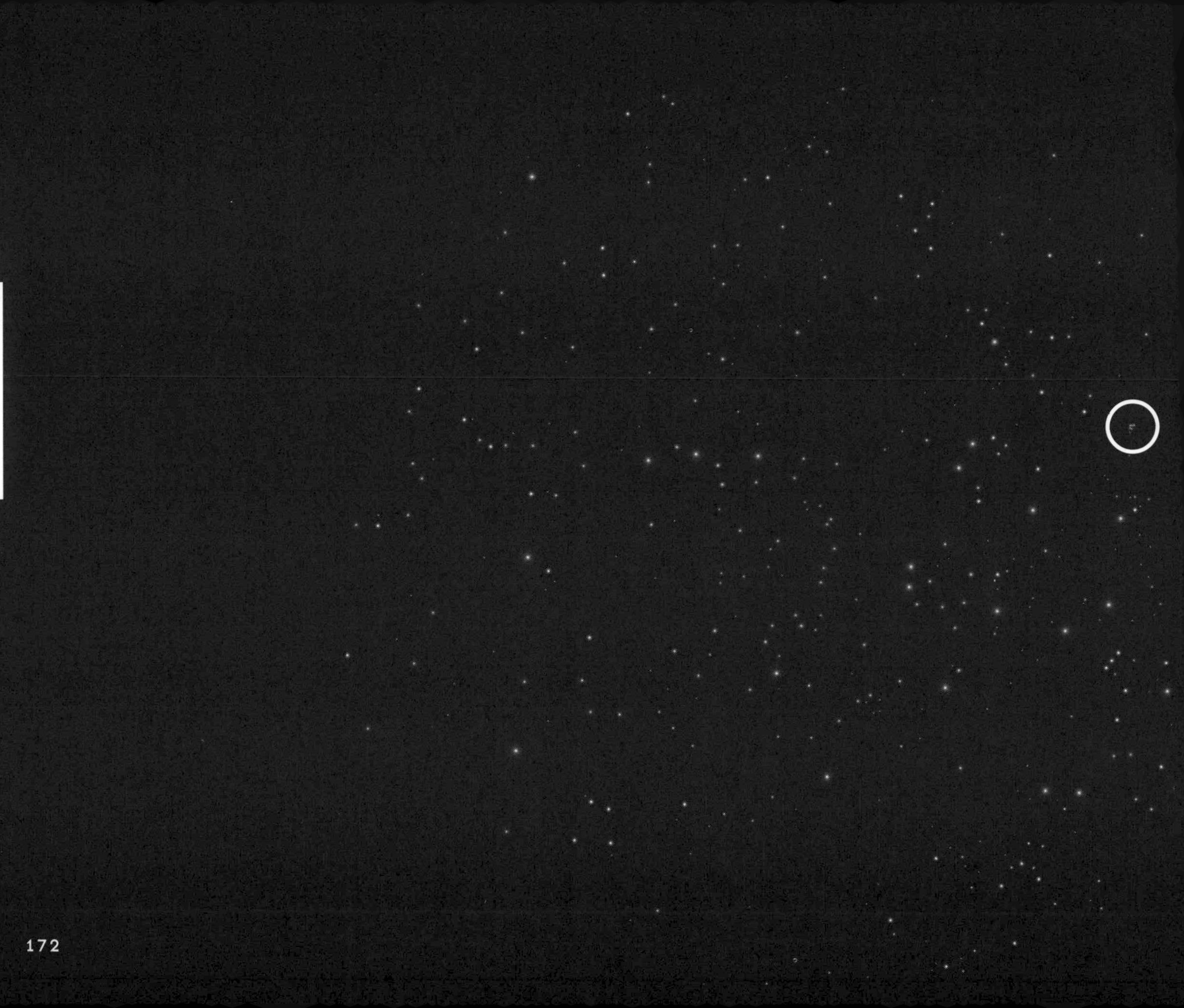

In this sky find Sirius, Orion,
Taurus and the Pleiades.

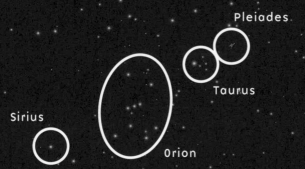

Sirius

Orion

Taurus

Pleiades

Roughly, where might you
expect to find a planet?

The planet line passes first
through Orion's hand and
then between Taurus and
the Pleiades.

A quick recap.

In this sky, find Polaris,
Cassiopeia and Cygnus.

This is a little tougher
than before, but that's
sometimes how things
are in the real sky.
Take your time.

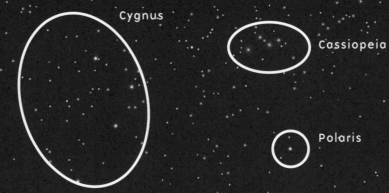

Cygnus

Cassiopeia

Polaris

And which of these
crosses is to the north?

The indigo bunting, a
type of finch, is thought
to recognize Polaris by
watching the other stars
rotate around it.

It then has a natural
compass (as you do)
to find its way north
in spring and south
for the winter.

The grand finale.

You should be able to
find six constellations
here and name them.

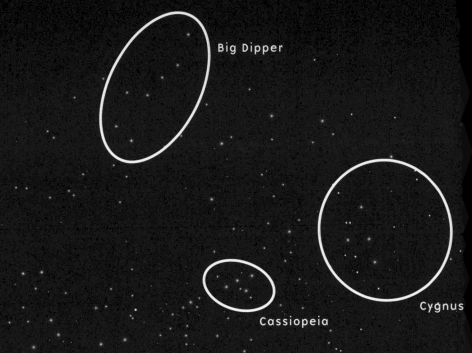

Big Dipper

Cygnus

Cassiopeia

Pleiades

Taurus

Orion

And you know four stars:
Betelgeuse, Sirius, Polaris,
and Vega.

Find them all.

Vega

Polaris

Betelgeuse

Sirius

Jupiter is visible in this
sky—where is it?

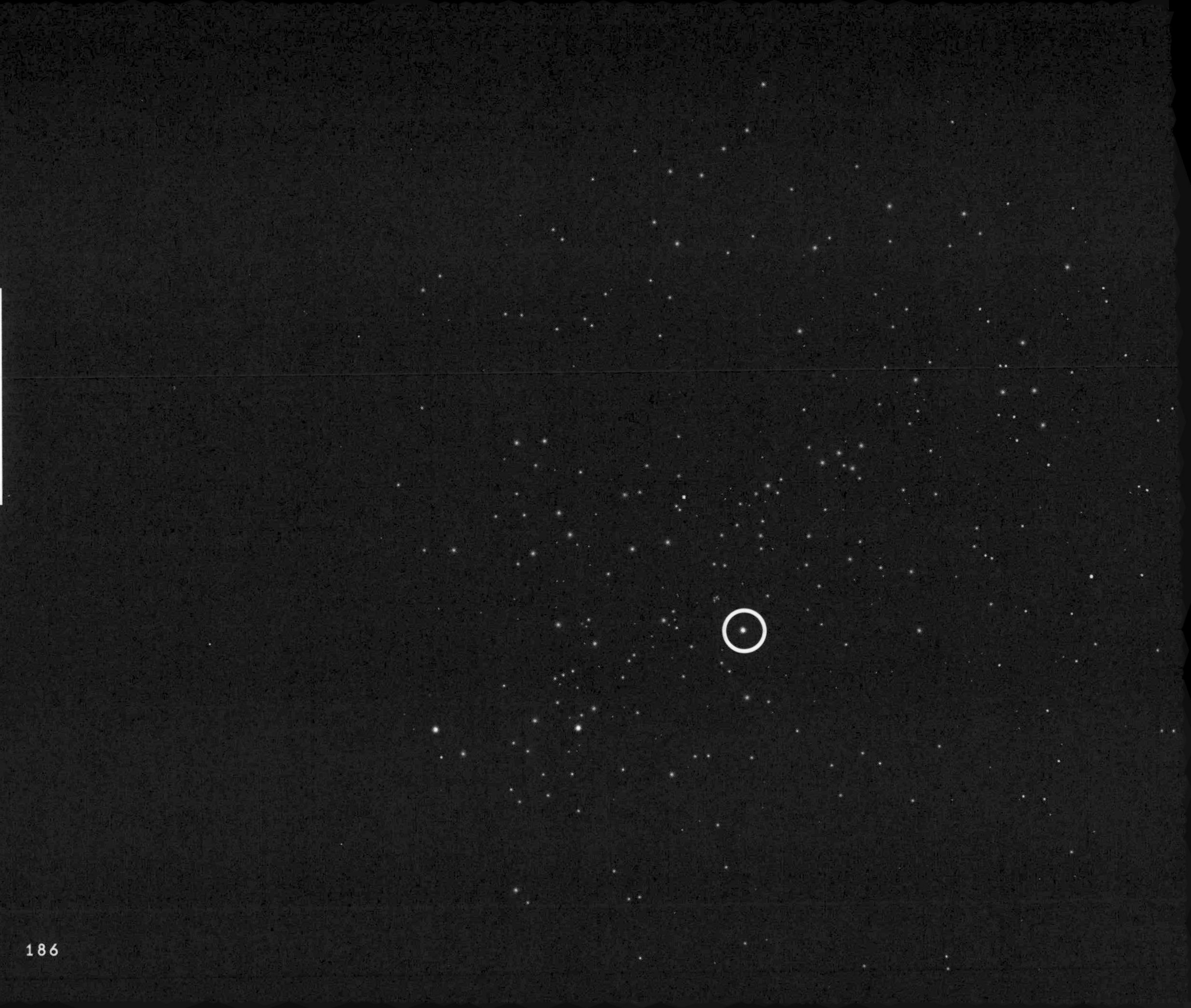

Where would you find
the Milky Way galaxy?

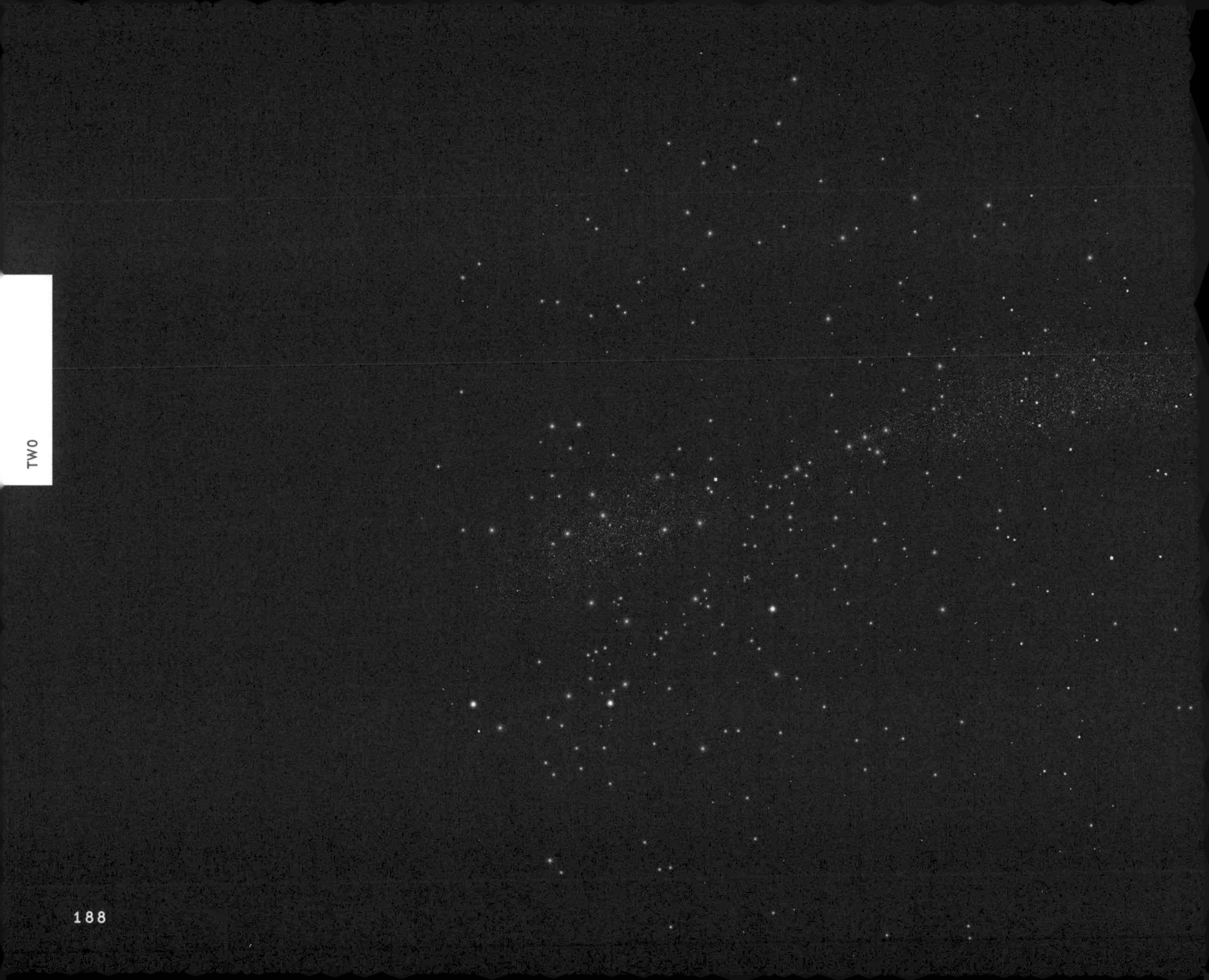

And which of these
points is north?

Six constellations, four stars,
a planet, a galaxy, and north.

You can safely say you
know your way around the
night skies.

You now know enough to
lead your own sight-seeing
tour of the sky.

Remember to practice in
the real sky within a week,
else your skills will fade.

Pause point

Take a break after reading this page.

As before, you'll get most from this book if you stop here and return a few days later. If possible, get some practice on the real sky in the meantime. There is a star map after page 234 you may find helpful.

The next section, the Epilogue, recaps everything you have learned so far. It doesn't introduce any new material; instead, it helps you hone your skills.

You know enough by now to find the Next Steps section, starting on page 229, interesting. It has pointers to a variety of resources you can use to build on the 'hooks' you have installed in your head so far.

Epilogue

The night sky changes throughout the year.

So, often you can see some constellations and not others.

But two constellations
are visible every night
(unless it's cloudy).

They are the two that are
visible here. Find them.

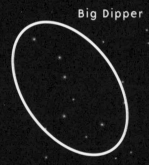

Big Dipper

Cassiopeia

Find Cygnus, the swan.

Find Vega.

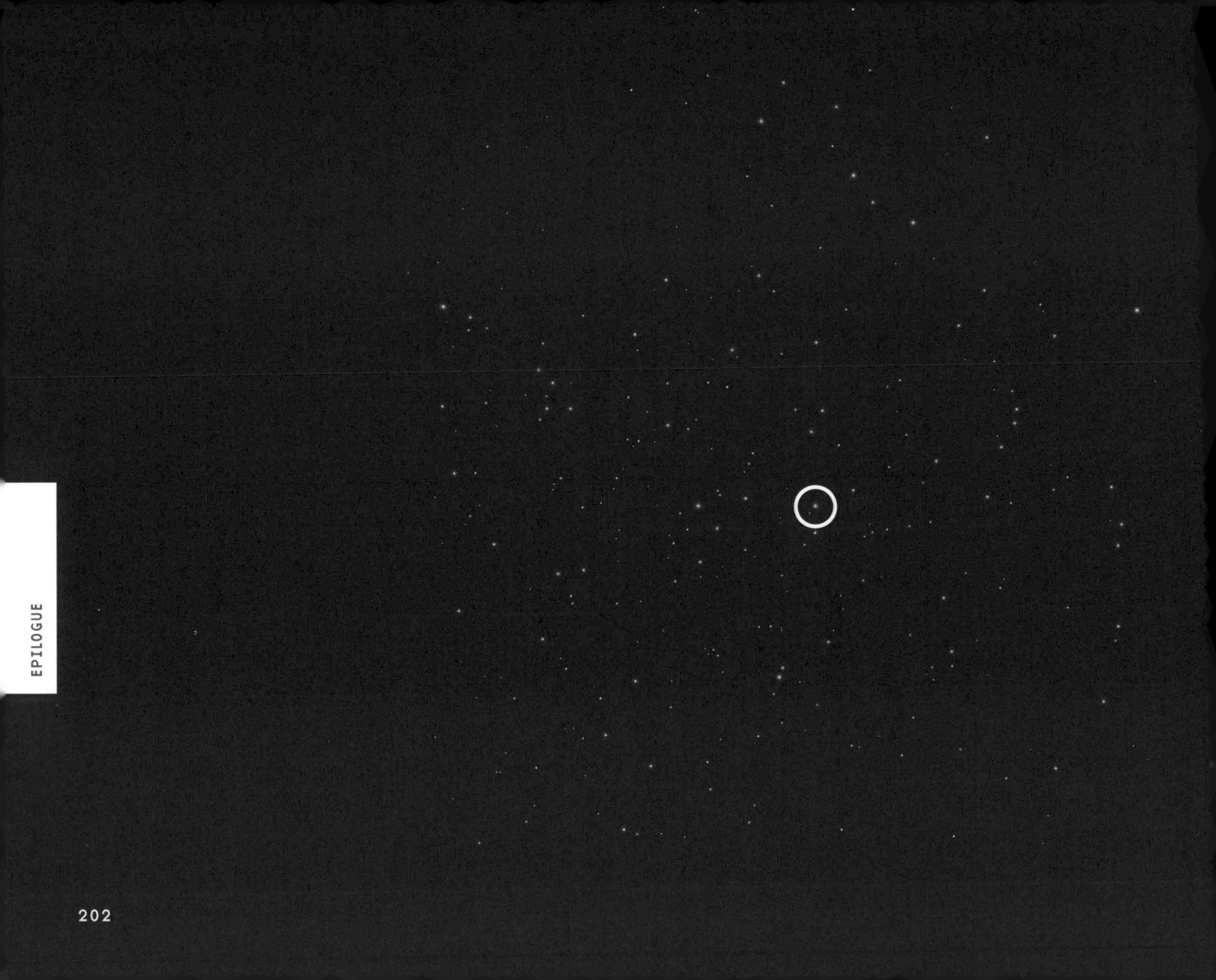

Now find the Big Dipper,
Polaris, Cassiopeia,
Cygnus and Vega.

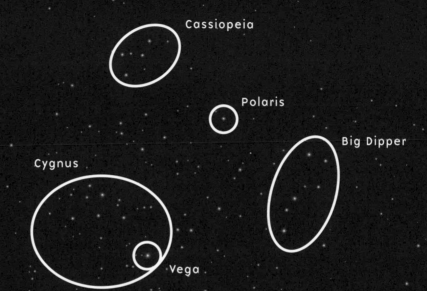

Cassiopeia

Polaris

Big Dipper

Cygnus

Vega

This group is typical
of what you can see
in a summer sky.

EPILOGUE

Often your view of the sky
will be obstructed—maybe
by buildings or trees.

Then you only have a
partial sky to work with.

Find a constellation in
this partial sky.

JON

Now find Sirius and
Betelgeuse.

Betelgeuse

Sirius

Find Taurus and
the Pleiades.

Pleiades

Taurus

Find a planet.

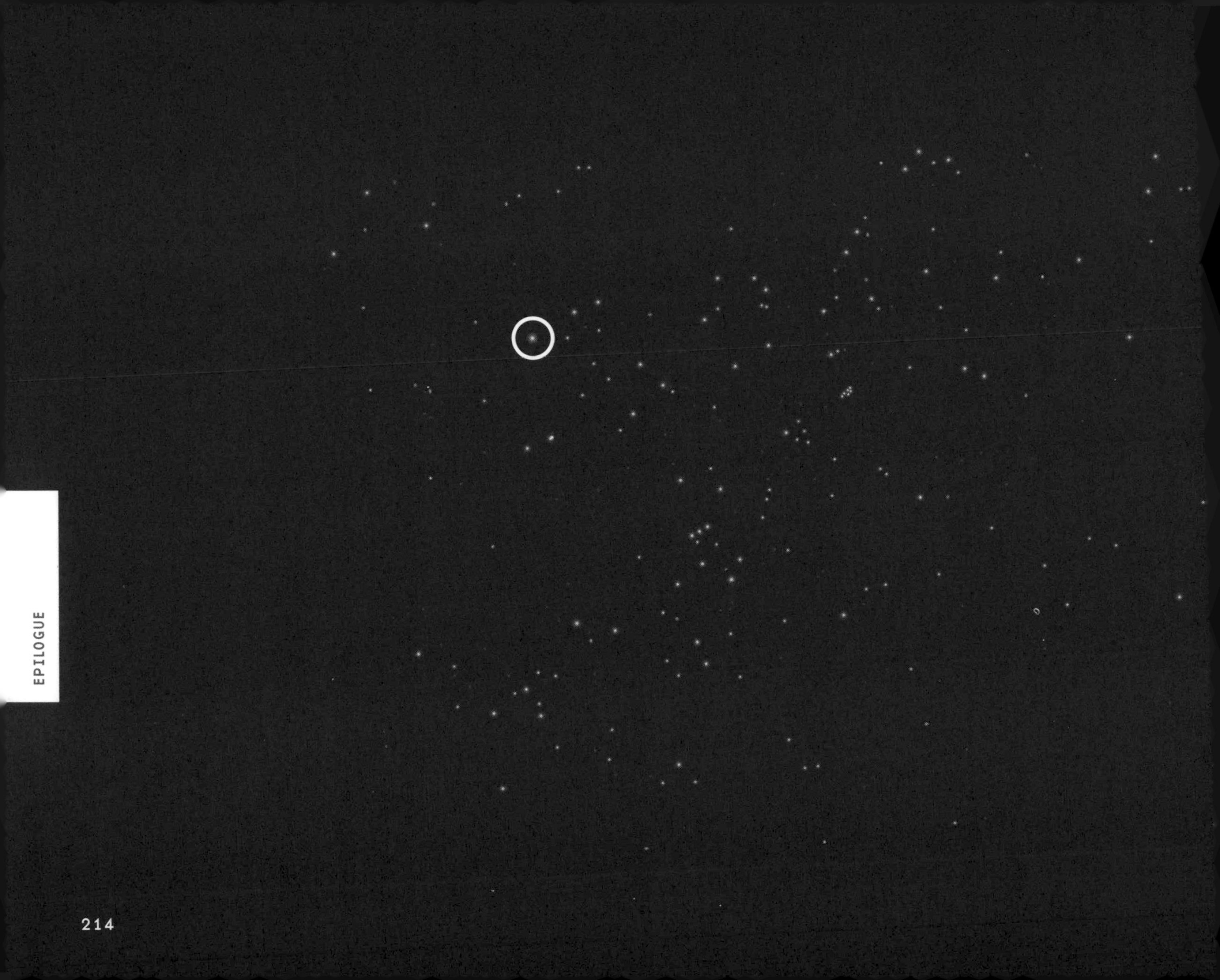

This group is typical of what
you can see in a winter sky.

Astronomers measure
distance in the sky
using a closed fist held at
arm's length (seriously).

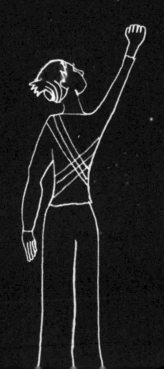

For instance, it's roughly two fists from Sirius to Orion's belt and another two to Taurus.

It's three fists from the
Big Dipper to Polaris;
another three to Cassiopeia;
and then another three-and-
a-half fists to Cygnus.

Of course, this is just a visual
aid—the stars are really
enormous distances apart.

While we're here,
where would you find
the Milky Way?

And which of these
points is north?

If you have read each page
up to this one, you will
never look at a night sky
the same way again.

View from New York City, USA, 2000 AD

There is, of course, much
more to it than we had the
space to cover.

But you have the beginnings
of a map in your head on
which to build.

Computed view from Qumran, Dead Sea, 1 AD

You have a window
onto the immensity
of our universe.

And you have a free
seat at the TV set of ancient
peoples.

Computed view from Stonehenge, England, 2000 BC

Thank you.

Computed view from Uruk, Mesopotamia, 4000 BC

Next Steps

Now that you know your way around the night sky, there is much more you can explore. We've included enough here to keep you busy and there is more at www.stikky.com/nightskies, which is updated frequently.

More stars and constellations

There are a total of 88 constellations in the sky, though not all are visible from the northern hemisphere. Here are some of the more famous ones, along with the brighter stars, for you to find on a star map and add to those you already know:

- *The Summer Triangle*, which is the three bright stars *Vega* (which you know), *Deneb* (the tail of Cygnus) and *Altair*

- *The Northern Crown* (*Corona Borealis* in Latin), a small arc of stars

- *Arcturus*, a bright star easily found by following the arc of the handle end of the *Big Dipper* a distance of three fists

- *Spica*, another bright star found by continuing the arc past *Arcturus* for another three fists

- *Bootes* (the Herdsman), the kite-shaped constellation with *Arcturus* as its brightest star

- The next easiest constellations:

  Lyra (*Vega* plus a small box)

  Cepheus (between *Cassiopeia* and *Cygnus*)

  Auriga (a box shape above *Orion*)

  Gemini (also above *Orion*).

Magazines

The two majors are:

- *Sky & Telescope*, at newsstands and online at www.skyandtelescope.com

- *Astronomy Magazine*, at newsstands and online at www.astronomy.com.

Star maps

One of the first things you should get hold of is a good map of the sky. We have provided two copies (so you can pull one out) after page 234. The view shown is typical of a winter sky in the United States or Europe.

- You can also get a 'planisphere' from most bookstores: a disk-shaped star map adjustable to any time and date

- www.fourmilab.ch/yoursky, www.skyviewcafe.com, and several other websites can draw the current sky for your location and time

- www.skymaps.com has a free, printable sky map, updated every month with current sky features

- www.seds.org has a comprehensive list of star mapping software packages including many that are free

- Probably the most popular commercial star mapping package is *Starry Night*
- There are several handy star maps for PDAs including *Planetarium*, *2sky*, and *Pocket Universe*.

Deep sky objects

For many people, the real attraction of the night sky is the experience of exploring 'deep sky' objects. To see them, you'll need binoculars or a telescope (see the next section).

Here are twelve of the most popular deep sky objects (not all are visible year round):

- *Albireo*, the most famous double star, a giant orange star orbited by a blue star at the head of *Cygnus*
- *Mizar* in the *Big Dipper*, an easy-to-find double star
- *Epsilon Lyrae*, the double-double near *Vega*
- *The Orion Nebula*, the most spectacular nebula (a huge cloud of gas where new stars are being minted), just below *Orion's* belt
- *The Pleiades*, a star cluster you already know how to find
- *The Milky Way*, our own galaxy (as you know) deserves a close look
- *The Great Globular Cluster* (officially known as M13), an estimated one million stars
- *The Dumbbell Nebula* (M27) not far from *Albireo*
- *The Lagoon Nebular* (M8) with a star cluster right next to it
- *The Andromeda Galaxy* (M31), the most distant object visible to the naked eye, conveniently pointed to by the second 'v' in *Cassiopeia's* 'w'
- *The Double Cluster* in the constellation *Perseus*
- *The Beehive*, a star cluster that resembles a swarm of bees.

Books that introduce deep sky objects include:

- *NightWatch* by Terence Dickinson
- *Turn Left at Orion* by Guy Consolmagno and Dan M Davis, which is more detailed and more dry
- The definitive three-volume *Burnham's Celestial Handbook* with as much detail as you could want, and then some.

If you want to get more serious about deep sky exploration, the *Astronomical League* (www.astroleague.org) runs a number of certification programs such as the Double Star Club in which you are challenged to find and log all the objects in a specially-compiled list.

Stargazing equipment

On a good night, you can see around 500 stars with the naked eye. With binoculars—even a small pair—you can see tens of thousands of stars and other objects. If you want to see greater detail, and you are willing to sacrifice some portability, you'll need a telescope.

The most common choice for astronomy **binoculars** is 7x50 which means a magnification of 7x and 50mm lenses. At higher power than 7x you'll need image stabilization technology, which is expensive, or a tripod. Bigger lenses than 50mm may be too heavy to hold for long. Before you buy, test the binoculars by finding a tiny object and viewing it at the edge of each lens—really excellent models will be sharp and undistorted right to the edge of the field of vision.

The **telescope** is an incredible invention: a few pieces of polished glass allow you to see hundreds of times better. But magnification, though hyped by manufacturers, is not the most important thing in a telescope. First, look for:

- A sturdy mount
- A large aperture (which collects more light and so provides a brighter image)
- Sharp optics, as for binoculars.

Star Ware by Philip Harrington is a comprehensive guide for the telescope buyer, and just about every book on astronomy includes guidance on buying a scope. The varying advice boils down to this:

- For $200 or less, buy binoculars instead; any telescope at this price runs a severe risk of being junk
- For around $500, buy a *Newtonian* reflector on a *Dobsonian* mount—a classic
- For $1000 and up, buy a *Maksutov-Cassegrain* or *Schmidt-Cassegrain*, both of which use a clever design that delivers a bigger aperture (good) with a shorter scope (good)
- If you're observing from somewhere with too much light pollution to see the *Milky Way* unaided, there's not much point in getting an aperture greater than 8 inches.

Purists turn their nose up at computerized 'go to' systems that point the telescope for you. You may prefer to invest instead in better optics, or you may think spending an hour finding an object manually is not your idea of fun.

Once you have your hardware, here are some tips to getting the most out of it:

- The principal thing you can do to improve your night vision is to let your eyes adjust to the dark for 15 minutes. If you use any light, make it red—for instance, put some red cloth over your flashlight
- You can pick out fainter objects by looking slightly away from them since your eye has more sensitive receptors away from its center
- It is almost impossible to locate a distant object by looking through the main telescope; use the finderscope (or the computer controller if you have one)
- Keep both eyes open, it's less tiring
- You may not see images as stunning as those from *Hubble*, but these photons are exclusively yours.

The Moon, the Sun and the planets

The **Moon's** features are sharpest along the line on its surface between light and dark, known as the 'terminator'. So the full moon (when bright light washes out its features) is in fact the worst time to view it. With a map you can find:

- *The Sea of Tranquility*, where man first set foot, assumed to be water by Galileo, but actually plains of hardened lava
- *Copernicus,* a massive crater, 17,000 feet deep

- *Tycho*, another crater, famous for the rays of moon soil surrounding it, some of them hundreds of miles long.

Observing the **Sun** obviously requires either a special filter or projection onto white card. You should be able to make out some sunspots: cooler areas on the sun's surface caused by powerful magnetic fields. Without more expensive filters, there's not much more to solar observation, though it has the distinct advantage of being something you can do when it's sunny.

Armed with binoculars or, preferably, a telescope, you can begin to explore our nearest neighbors. As you know, **planets** move along a line, called the 'ecliptic', above *Orion's* arm and between *Taurus* and the *Pleiades*. All eight official planets in the solar system (*Pluto's* status is disputed) are visible with a telescope. Highlights include:

- Tracking a moon of *Jupiter* across the planet's multi-colored cloud belts and huge red spot
- *Saturn's* rings composed of hunks of ice, dazzling even across a billion kilometers of space
- *Uranus* or *Neptune*, just so you can say you've seen them.

Night sky events

The constellations and deep sky objects are always there (if not always visible because the Earth is in the way). Against this backdrop the sky also hosts a large number of special events: artificial satellites spinning past, auroras, comets, eclipses, meteors, and supernovas. It's a busy sky if you know where to look.

You can see many of the **artificial objects** we have sent into space. The wonderful website www.heavens-above.com tells you when the International Space Station, the Space Shuttle, and hundreds of other artificial satellites are visible from any location on Earth.

An **aurora** is a spectacular but intermittent phenomenon caused by the 'wind' of particles from the Sun creating beautiful shifting patterns in the night sky. You have to be as far north as Alaska, or as far south as Australia, to see one.

An asteroid is just a very small planet, usually too small to see. **Comets** are much more interesting for observers: dirty snowballs of ice and rock orbiting the Sun with a long tail of dust and gas. For information on visible comets see the *International* [sic] *Comet Quarterly* at http://cfa-www.harvard.edu/icq/icq.html. If you are worried about comets and asteroids on a collision course with the Earth (none are known of at the time of writing), visit http://impact.arc.nasa.gov to find out what the United States government is doing about it.

Solar eclipses—when the Moon comes between the Earth and the Sun—are rare. On average there is less than one total eclipse per year and you have to travel thousands of miles to get a good view. The next total eclipse visible from North America is in 2017 and Europe has to wait until 2026. But a total eclipse is such a cult event it is worth seeing once in your life. (Lunar eclipses—when the Earth comes between the Sun and the Moon and so casts its shadow on the Moon—are equally infrequent and much less dramatic.) Here are the upcoming total solar eclipses (predictions by Fred Espenak, NASA/GFSC, details at http://sunearth.gsfc.nasa.gov/eclipse/):

- 2003, November 23 over Antarctica
- 2005, April 8 over the South Pacific
- 2006, March 29 over North Africa and Turkey
- 2008, August 1 over the Arctic and Siberia
- 2009, July 22 over China and India
- 2010, July 11 over the South Pacific
- 2012, November 13 over Northern Australia
- 2013, November 3 over Central Africa
- 2015, March 20 over the Arctic
- 2016, March 9 over Indonesia
- 2017, August 21 over the United States
- 2019, July 2 over Chile and Argentina
- 2020, December 14 over Chile and Argentina
- 2021, December 4 over Antarctica
- 2023, April 20 over Indonesia and Australia
- 2024, April 8 over Mexico, United States, and Canada
- 2026, August 12 over Iceland and Spain
- 2027, August 2, over North Africa, Southern Europe, and the Middle East.

A **meteor**—the streak of light produced by a small particle burning up in the Earth's atmosphere—can be seen any night but you may have to watch for up to an hour. The less patient can improve the odds dramatically by observing during a meteor storm when you could see several per minute. The main storms happen the same time every year and last a few days around the dates below. Their names tell you where to look (ie, *Orionids* near *Orion*, *Taurids* near *Taurus*).

- January 4, *Quadrantids*
- April 22, *Lyrids*
- May 5, *Eta Aquarids*
- July 29, *Delta Aquarids*
- August 12, *Perseids*
- October 21, *Orionids*
- November 18, *Leonids*
- December 14, *Geminids.*

You can find more details on meteor storms at the website of the *American Meteor Society*, www.amsmeteors.org.

The most spectacular night sky event would be a **supernova**, when a star explodes. The last known supernova in our galaxy was in 1680 and was actually quite dim. No-one knows when the next might be.

You can get a regular email highlighting celestial events called the *Skywatcher's Bulletin* at www.skyandtelescope.com. The excellent site www.astronomydaily.com provides a calendar or upcoming events customized for your location. And the definitive annual reference book for North American skies is the *Observer's Handbook* published by the Royal Astronomical Society of Canada.

Clubs, parties, observatories

There are hundreds of astronomy **clubs** in the United States, transforming stargazing into a social activity. They offer regular gatherings with guided observations, sometimes at observatories. About 200 of them are members of *The Astronomical League* at www.astroleague.org.

Searching the web for 'star party' will throw up dozens of annual conventions and **parties** each year such as:

- *Stellafane* in Vermont
- *Astrofest* in Illinois
- *Starfest* in New York
- *The Grand Canyon Star Party* in Arizona
- *The Texas Star Party*.

Of the dozens of US **observatories**, only a handful will let you peer through their telescope:

- *Lick Observatory*, California, www.ucolick.org
- *Chabot Observatory*, California, www.cosc.org
- *Leander McCormick Observatory*, Virginia, www.astro.virginia.edu
- *Allegheny Observatory*, Pennsylvania, www.pitt.edu/~aobsvtry
- *Dearborn Observatory*, Illinois, www.astro.nwu.edu
- *Yerkes Observatory*, Illinois, http://astro.uchicago.edu/yerkes
- *Lowell Observatory*, Arizona, www.lowell.edu
- *Steward Observatory Astronomy Camp*, Arizona, www.as.arizona.edu/steward
- *Pine Mountain Observatory*, Oregon, http://pmo-sun.uoregon.edu.

Stikky recommended websites

There are hundreds of websites related to the night skies. Here are a few more of our favorites:

- www.exploratorium.com, possibly the world's best online museum
- http://setiathome.ssl.berkeley.edu, the SETI@home project lets your computer help in the search for extraterrestrial intelligence
- http://skyview.gsfc.nasa.gov, a virtual telescope, perfect for cloudy nights
- http://hubblesite.org, pictures from the greatest telescope ever built
- http://www.hps.cam.ac.uk/starry/starrymessenger.html, Cambridge University's history of astronomy
- For online message boards of like-minded people go to http://groups.yahoo.com or www.google.com/grphp and search for astronomy.

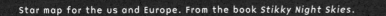
Star map for the US and Europe. From the book *Stikky Night Skies*.

The Big Dipper

Vega

Polaris

Cygnus

Cassiopeia

Pleiades

Taurus

Sirius   Orion

Star map for the us and Europe. From the book *Stikky Night Skies*.

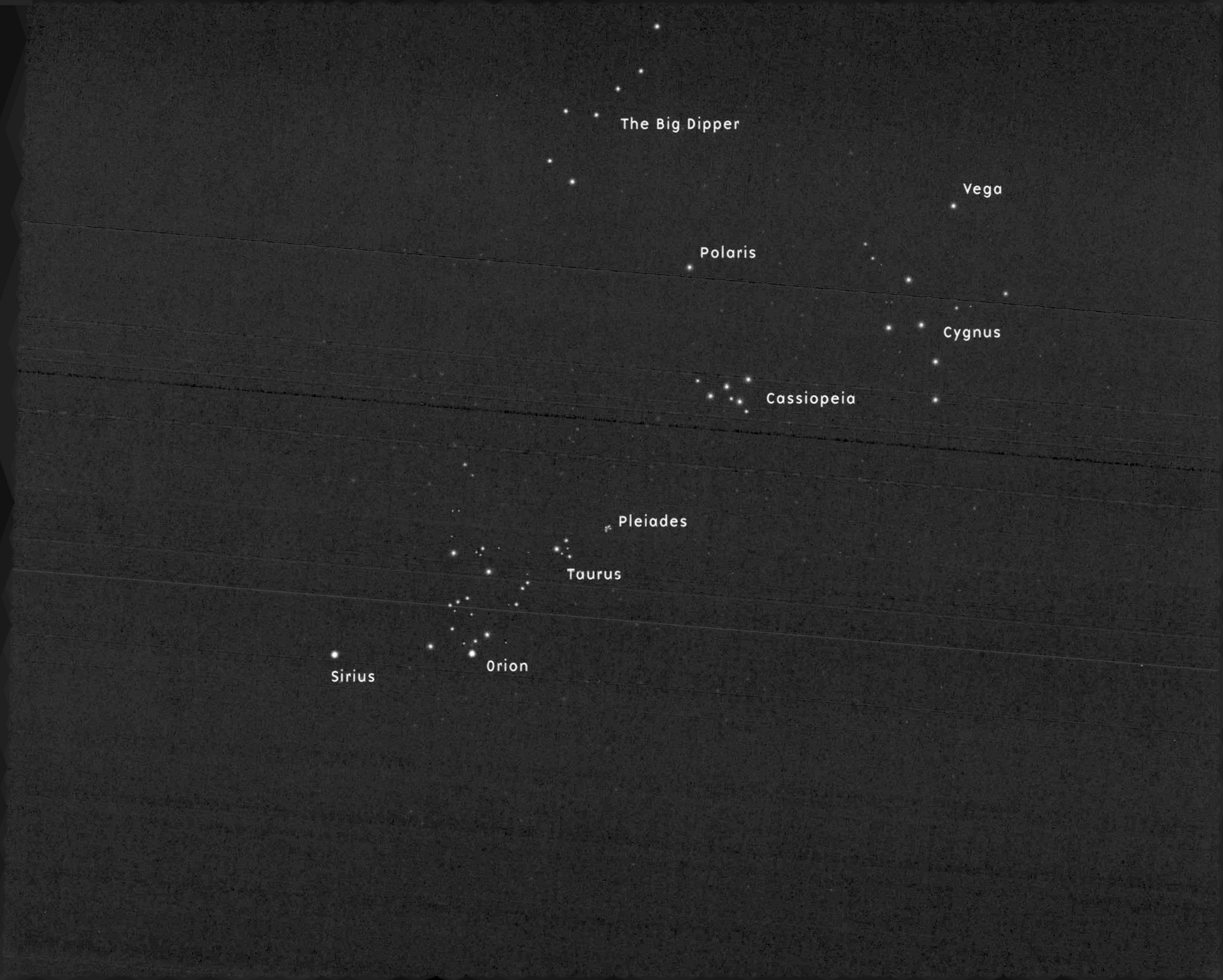
The Big Dipper
Vega
Polaris
Cygnus
Cassiopeia
Pleiades
Taurus
Sirius
Orion

About Stikky books

The Stikky story

We started publishing Stikky books in 2003 after a web-based trial generated far more interest than we expected. Our first book (the one you're holding) took a year to create.

The series covers topics we believe will be of value and interest to anyone. We created it because we couldn't find a 'how to' book that takes into account recent findings about how people learn. Instead, they often provide too much information and structure it in a way that makes sense to experts but not to beginners. According to our research, most people read less than half of 'how to' books they buy.

The Stikky approach

- Start with small pieces of knowledge and systematically build them into a comprehensive picture
- Make the practice environment as similar as possible to the real world
- Organize the topic around readers' goals such as: Which way is north?
- Provide plenty of practice—80% of learning is really re-learning so we stage multiple opportunities to test and reinforce your knowledge
- Make it fun.

How we create a Stikky book

Each book is prepared with the help of domain experts, some of whom are named on the cover. It goes through multiple rounds of review by Test Readers (if you would like to become a Stikky Test Reader, visit www.stikky.com). We record every time they get stuck, together with hundreds of other suggestions, and make careful changes. Then we go through the whole process again.

Everything about the product in your hands was informed by this research: the format, the binding, even the name. And we only publish a book when we know it works.

Our charity pledge

We promise to spend 10% of profits from the series on knowledge-based charity. We believe that knowledge generates independence and so is a liberating form of aid.

Upcoming Stikky books

Future titles will cover topics such as playing an instrument or diet and nutrition. If there are topics you would like to see included in the series, suggest them at www.stikky.com, where you will also find news of additions to the series before publication.

What our readers say

A fantastic learning experience. Thank you, thank you, thank you. Now I can look up and see. *JP, USA*

What a magnificent idea! I will email everybody I know that even MIGHT be interested! Please PLEASE create more of these. *DJ, Ohio*

I put my 11-year-old and 7-year-old through it and we went out and viewed the sky afterwards, it made for a wonderful evening event. *SL, Massachusetts*

This has been the easiest way for me to learn constellations than all the pictures I have looked at in the past few weeks. *PW, Melbourne, Australia*

Thank you SO much for making things so easy. I feel like I've made a start, at long last. *CW, England*

Now I can observe and understand with confidence. Thank you so much. *LC, Michigan*

We need more teachers/educators like you with this approach. *JF, USA*

Beautifully simple, entertaining and delightful. *PL, Ontario*

After running through the sequence, I was able to locate all the points very quickly, can't wait until tomorrow to try it out, outside. *PP, Sydney, Australia*

Just read the sequence. Heading out to stargaze even as you read. Many thanks and congratulations. *RS, Australia*

I am a behavior analyst who works with handicapped kids. I would like to thank you for providing this easy way for beginners to get oriented and find their way around the night sky. *RCL, Illinois*

Thank you for this stimulating yet effective course. Within 15 minutes not only could I navigate, I could easily locate all of the constellations shown to me. *PL, USA*

I have tried to learn constellations in the night sky for years—may I use this for teaching my students? *SH, Kansas*

Thank You

Susanne Agerbak · Janice Ball · Quentin Ball · Ray Ball · Jonathan Bloom · Jonas Bordo · Victoria Cable-Kulli · Audrey Carney
Helen Crawley · Simon Darling · Merry Davis · Colleen Helmken · Andrew Lyons · Alix Martin · Nell Montgomery · John Oakes
Earle Sandberg · Ryan Sanders · Jo Seaton · Paula Simchak · Clare Smith · Leah Souffrant · Linda Steinman · Kirsteen White